CHINA, ITS PEOPLE AND LIFE

外国人，中国情

著 | Lisa Carducci
李莎·卡尔杜齐

译 | Yu Lan
于岚

五洲传播出版社
CHINA INTERCONTINENTAL PRESS

Contents

Introduction 6
Kind people in Qinghai 8
Play the game at Panjiayuan 14
Authentic fakes 18
China, and the rest of the world 22
Capitalizing on wrong values 26
Learning Chinese, such an exploit! 30
The pajama dilemma 34
South Korea was so different! 38
To be late without losing face 48
Those who deserve it 52
In the name of the animals 56
Public transportation as a textbook 64
Dog regulation necessary 68
Lunar New Year gains in status 72
A city without peddlers 78
Questioning retirement age 82
To be or not to be a Tiger Mother 86
Desks, blackboards and textbooks? It's not Montessori 92
Smell the roses in our Chinese garden 100

目录

前 言 7
青海多好人 9
趣游潘家园 15
正宗的假货 19
中国与世界 23
生财无道 27
中文好难学 31
睡衣困境 35
韩国如此不同 39
迟到却没丢面子 49
那些值得尊重的人 53
以动物的名义 57
我的公交大课堂 65
养狗需要立规矩 69
春节地位节节高 73
没有小贩的城市 79
也谈退休年龄 83
子女教育说“虎妈” 87
蒙台梭利教育理念的真谛 93
墙内开花自有香 101

Is overseas study boom hurting China's schools? 106
Do you return home for Xmas? 112
About translation 118
Not drunk, but… 126
My dream of Taiwan 132
Relativity is not exclusively Einstein's matter 138
A taste for luxury goods 142
Free, safe, and doubly efficient 146
Painting a pretty picture when speaking Chinese 150
Resident not the same as citizen 154
No waste: good news! 160

留学海外与立足本土……107
要回家过圣诞吗？……113
谈翻译……119
谈谈中国的酒文化……127
我的台湾梦……133
这里也有相对论……139
奢侈品之惑……143
“院士”助戒烟……147
作画与说中文……151
居民并非公民……155
喜闻节约厉行……161

Introduction

For two decades, I have followed the evolution of China on the spot. I have lived at her rhythm, enjoyed her success and cried with her when disasters struck.

All that time, I have expressed my views in books, such as the series *Talking About China* (I, II and III). The series proceeds under a new title, with articles published between 2010 and 2013 on *China Daily, Beijing Review, People's Daily Overseas Edition, China.org*, etc.. Limited by a set length when published in the newspapers, the texts may have been modified in this book to give a deeper insight. Some articles have been written especially for the present collection.

Topics cover moral values, urbanization, education, translation, animals' rights, retirement, etc., in short, life and society, and situations in China and in Western countries, as this book aims at Chinese and non-Chinese readers as well.

No matter what I write, I always write only what I think.

Lisa Carducci

前　言

二十多年来，我亲历了中国的发展变化。我生活在中国的节拍中，分享她的成功，也曾为她受到的灾难而流泪。

其间，我写了许多有关中国的观感，先后在英文《中国日报》《北京周报》以及《人民日报》海外版、中国网等媒体发表，并曾以《一个西方人眼中的中国》（1–3）系列将2010年到2013年发表的文章集辑出版。有的文章在报纸发表时有篇幅限制，为使读者有更深刻的理解，收入本书时作了一些修改。另外有些文章则是专为本书写作的。

本书的文章内容五花八门，涉及社会道德、城市化、教育、翻译、动物，退休等诸多话题，涵盖了社会和生活的许多方面，不但涉及中国，也涉及西方国家。因此，本书中国读者可以读，外国人也可以看。

笔落行文，我写我心。

李莎·卡尔杜齐

Kind people in Qinghai

Qinghai was my last Chinese province to visit in 2003. I have returned three more times, and each visit added to the number of kind persons I met there.

On my first visit, when in Xunhua Sala'ar Autonomous Xian, a mad man rushed at me and pushed me strongly. I fell in the dust but was not hurt. I could not hold it against him as he suffered mental disease. Several persons came to help, and a Sala'ar woman invited me to her home for refreshing and resting. Then, she accompanied me to a small restaurant and offered me a bowl of handmade noodles, as only Muslims can do. The butcher who had witnessed the accident from his shop came to ask for news, and offered to accompany me to a hospital if I needed.

In Xining, I needed a map but didn't know where to buy it. I asked a passer-by, who was a Tibetan. He could speak local Chinese dialect a little but I couldn't. He took me by the sleeve and accompanied me to a faraway Xinhua Bookstore. There, he didn't leave before making sure I had found what I wanted.

In Tongren Xian, I was very tired after walking a whole day. I could not find anyone speaking Chinese *putonghua*, let apart Italian, French or English. Finally I saw a sign: 茶馆, Tea House. How nice it was to sit and rest! But more than a businessman, it is a friend that I found. A Tibetan University student was back home from summer holidays and was helping his sister-in-law with the tea house. Though he had a very strong accent in Chinese, we chatted for two hours while having *suyou cha* (butter tea) and he didn't let me leave without a big bag of *qingke* (barley flour) and a large piece of butter, so I could make my own *suyou* cha back in Beijing. We remained friends until now.

青海多好人

青海是我 2003 年在中国访问的最后一个省。后来，我又去过三次，每次都遇到了好人。

我第一次去那里的时候，在循化撒拉族自治县，一个疯子冲过来对我用力地推推搡搡。我倒在泥土里，但是没有受伤。我不能怨他，因为他有精神病。几个人过来帮助我。一个撒拉族妇女请我到她家休息一下。然后，她带我去了一家饭馆，给我买了一碗只有穆斯林才会做的手擀面。一个肉店师傅从店里目睹了事情经过后跑过来问情况，说如果需要的话，他可以陪我去医院。

在西宁，我需要一张地图，但是不知道去哪里买。我向一个过路的藏族人打听。他能讲一点当地的方言，可是我听不懂。他拉着我的袖子，陪着我走了很远的路才找到一家新华书店。他在那里一直等到我买到我所需要的东西后才走。

在同仁县，我走了一天，感觉很累。我找不到会说普通话的人，更别提会说意大利语、法语或者英语的了。最后，我看到一个牌子，上面写着“茶馆”，能够坐进去歇歇真好！我在那里结识的不只是一个老板，后来他还成了我的朋友。他是一个藏族大学生，放暑假在家帮助嫂子照料茶馆的生意。我们边喝酥油茶边聊天。虽然他的汉话口音很重，我们还是聊了两个钟头。我走的时候，他非要送给我一大袋青稞和一大块奶油，让我回北京后可以在家里自己做酥油茶。直到现在，我们也还是朋友。

Then I met Zhang Jun who not only was a skilled driver but a dedicated and honest man, not money-oriented but who liked to "serve" his clients. He showed me things that I could never discover by myself such as a cascade hidden in the mountain; he brought me to the home of the late 10th Panchen Lama, and on the morning of my departure, he came to pick me up at my hotel for free and didn't leave the bus station before making sure I was on the right bus.

On another visit, a Mongol ethnic woman offered me her apartment in Xining, but as she was in Beijing at that moment, she called her neighbor and told her to give me the key. We had just met, and she trusted me to that point? I was really moved.

On my third visit, a seller of knee-protectors recognized me, at the market, and said last time I had paid for three pairs and taken only two. He was right. But I had never expected him to give me one pair for free, as it was my error.

This year, I went to spend the *Losar* festival with the family of a university student I support financially. The five family members called me Ani (aunt) in Tibetan. The evening before I left, the mother prepared a large bread for me to bring back. The daughter and her father not only accompanied me from their village to the bus station in Tongren, but stayed with me until I could find a bus, what wasn't easy on *Chu san* (the third day of the new year).

Then I visited another girl I support for study. She lives in Minhe Xian, a Hui and Tu Autonomous Xian, but their village is inhabited exclusively by Han. Every family member showed respect and kindness to me. Not only three meals including pork, chicken, beef and fish were prepared for me within a few hours, but when I left, a relative offered to drive me to the bus station at one hour from the village, and finally drove me up to Xining, and didn't want to be paid.

But I will never forget what happened to me recently. On the bus from Jainca to Ping'an, I gave my seat to a woman with a toddler. Trying to keep balance, I put my notebook on the upper shelve with my gloves and a *tangkha*. When I got off, I forgot my notebook,

后来，我遇到了张军。他不但是一个熟练的司机，也是一个热心工作和诚实的人。他不是那种财迷心窍的人，而是热心为顾客提供真正的服务。他带我看的地方，比如山里的瀑布等，我自己根本不可能发现。他还带我去看了十世班禅喇嘛的旧居。我离开的那天早上，他免费来旅馆接我，直到我上对了汽车才离开车站。

还有一次，在西宁有一个蒙古族妇女让我住在她的公寓里。当时她人在北京。她给邻居打电话，让她们把钥匙转交给我。我们才认识不久，她竟然这么相信我！我真的被感动了。

我第三次去西宁，一个在市场上卖羊毛护膝的人认出了我，说我上次付了三付护膝的钱而只拿了两付。他没有说错，可是我没想到他这次果真会免费给我一付，因为上次是我自己的问题，不是他的责任。

今年，我去了我资助的一个藏族大学生仁青卓玛的家，跟她全家一起过藏历新年。她家里五口人，都管我叫“阿尼”，藏语就是“阿姨”的意思。我离开的前一天晚上，卓玛的妈妈给我准备了一大块面包让我带着。走的时候，卓玛和她爸爸把我从家送到车站，而且等到我找到汽车后才走。

后来，我去民和县看望我资助的另外一个女孩李凤连。民和县是一个回族土族自治县，但是他们村里住的都是汉族。村里每个家庭都对我礼貌有加，和善可亲。几个小时内他们给我准备了丰盛的三餐，有猪肉、鸡肉、牛肉和鱼。我离开的时候，他们一个亲戚主动开车开了一个小时把我送到汽车站，后来干脆把我送到西宁，没有要我一分钱。

不过，最近发生的一件事让我最难忘。在尖扎到平安的长途车上，我把座位让给了一个带小孩的妇女。为了站稳，我把我的笔记本、手套和一张唐卡放在车里的行李架上。可是我下车的时候却忘了拿笔记本。

which contained the notes of several interviews, phone numbers, data of my hotel in Xining, and of my return flight to Beijing. I was desperate.

The next day, when I reached Xining, I rushed to the bus station. An employee said: "If you don't know the car's number, there is no way out", as buses have irregular schedule, but he had compassion for me and he introduced me to the wonderful Ms. Wei. Sometimes it pays to be a foreigner...

"Don't worry, within 48 hours your notebook will be here," said the woman. But I was leaving the next morning.

After several calls and patient explanations, Wei Suxia finally traced the bus, and the driver Ma Jianxiong and his assistant Zhao Ersha. But the men, both Hui, were off that day. Wei convinced them of the notebook's importance for me, and the good hearted Ma and Zhao decided to return to Xining to hand the precious notebook to me. This is the most touching event of my four trips to Qinghai.

笔记本里有我几次采访的笔记、联系电话、西宁旅馆的资料，还有回京航班的资料。我简直绝望了。

第二天，我到西宁以后，马上去长途车站寻找。一个保安说："没有车牌号码，没有希望找到那辆车。"因为一辆长途车跑的班次是不固定的。他很同情我的遭遇，把我介绍给了魏素霞，一个非常好的人。

"没关系"，她说，"你的笔记本48小时之内就会回到这里。"可是，我第二天就得离开啊！

魏素霞打了许多电话，耐心地向对方解释事情的经过，终于帮我联系到当天那辆长途车的司机马健雄和售票员赵二沙。他们两个人都是回民，不巧那天都不当班。魏素霞告诉他们，这个笔记本对我非常重要。马师傅和赵师傅都是好心人，决定开回西宁将笔记本给我送回来。四次青海之行，这是最让我感动的一件事。

Play the game at Panjiayuan

After two decades in China, "bargaining" remains my favorite game. At Panjiayuan, Beijing, I was looking for a bronze Buddha's hand. I first visited the small shops around the market, stopping only where bronze pieces could be seen. A man followed me; he addressed me in English. I smiled without answering, keeping my Chinese as a trump for later.

In the shop, the saleswoman had something interesting, but I wanted to see other shops too. She opened the door to let me out, the man asked her: "What does she want to buy?" I answered before her, "*Wo yijing maile, xiexie nide guanxin.* (I already bought, thanks for your care.)" He understood I was not a newcomer and he would get no commission bringing a customer to the right shop.

In the section where merchandise is spread on the ground, I used only my eyes to detect a Buddha's hand. The merchants fixed my eyes but could not guess what I was looking for. I remained silent as I didn't want them to show me all kinds of Buddha statues. "What does the lady want?" they asked each other. I heard hundreds of "Look-a-look" but was not drawn by the hand or by vendors' arms around my shoulders as it happens in other markets.

In the fourth row, I stopped in front of a tea pot, a kind I don't have in my collection, but heard a little voice inside: "You have no room for more teapots!" Aware of my interest, and all the following vendors offered me their teapots.

I continued to walk slowly, eyes on a possible Buddha's hand, until I saw the most finely crafted pair of chopsticks, another article

趣游潘家园

在中国住了20年，“讨价还价”仍然是我喜欢的游戏。有一次，在北京的潘家园旧货市场，我想买一个青铜的佛手。我先去市场附近的小店，只看卖青铜器的。一个男的跟着我，用英语跟我说话。我只是笑笑，把中文留作我最后的王牌。

在一个店里，老板娘有一件有趣的东西，不过我也想看看别的店。她打开门放我出去。那个男人问她：“她想买什么？”我抢在老板娘前头用中文说:“我已经买了。谢谢你的关心。”他明白了我不是头一回来，他不可能在我身上赚拉客的回扣。

在小贩商品散布的地摊上，我只用眼睛搜寻佛手。卖东西的盯着我的眼睛，可是看不出来我要买什么。我一言不发，免得他们都拿佛像给我看。“那个女的要买什么？”我听见他们互相打听。在潘家园我上百次听到过“可以看看，看看吧”，可是从来没有像在别的市场那样，被小贩拉住或者勾住肩膀强迫看他卖的东西。

我在第四排一个茶壶前边停下来。这种茶壶我的收藏里没有，可是我心里有个声音悄悄在说：“你家里已经没有地方放更多的茶壶了！”看出了我的兴趣所在，后面的小贩都把茶壶拿给我看。

我继续慢慢往前走，眼睛搜寻着佛手。这时候我看见一双制作精美

I collect. At that point I decided to open my mouth. I thought they were ivory chopsticks but didn't want to play all my cards at once. "How much for your *bone* chopsticks?" I asked in Chinese? After a short hesitation, the man showed three fingers. "Three hundred, hmm?" "Three thousands," he replied, "This is ivory!" "Sorry, I can't buy such expensive articles," I said putting them back. The vendor would not let me go so easily. He asked how much I wanted to pay; I said I didn't want to buy. In fact, when buying antiques, I think there is no standard price, but a subjective value that is the price the collector feels reasonable for the degree of pleasure obtained from possessing the object.

Two alleys further, I saw the chopsticks-man beside me, asking again how much I would pay. I tried to ignore him but he insisted and became very boring. I finally said "200" in a way to get rid of him. He smiled slyly but didn't surrender! Several steps later he asked again, and I said I already answered his question. "Can you rise a little?" I just turned a deaf ear to him. "Okay, 200," he accepted.

As he had come down to my price, I should have bought; this is the market rule: Never announce a price if you have no intention to buy. But actually, the seller had not played a fair game. I told him: "As you so easily dropped from 3,000 to 200 yuan, how can I believe you? Now, I know this is bone, not ivory. Sorry! Had you started at 400, it would have been different. Trying to trick the customer this way, you play against yourself."

However it was not over yet. I had seen all the merchandise except the Buddha's hand I wanted, and was leaving. Another man appeared, with a pair of chopsticks in his hands. "These are mine, not that man's" he said pointing at the former vendor. In fact, this man's chopsticks were not even bone but plastic ones.

的筷子。这也是我要收藏的。这时候我决定开口。我觉得是象牙的，但是我不想把我的底牌都亮出来。“你这种骨筷怎么卖？”我问道。那个人犹豫了一下，伸出三个手指头。“三百？”我问。“三千，”他说，“这是象牙的！”“对不起，我买不起这么贵的东西，”我说着把东西放回去了。那个小贩不肯轻易放过我，他问我愿意付多少钱。我说我不想买了。实际上，我认为买古玩没有标准的价格，只有主观的价值，那就是收藏家觉得能给他带来快乐的东西值得他付多少钱。

转了两排摊位后，那个卖筷子的又来到我身旁，问我愿意付多少钱。我不想理他，可是他继续纠缠，到了烦人的地步。为了打发他，我就说：“两百。”听到这个，他一脸鬼笑，仍然不肯罢手！走了几步后他又问我。我说我已经回答你的问题了。“你能不能多给点？”我装没听见。“好吧，两百就两百。”他说。

现在他把价格降到我出的价位了，我就应该买。这是市场的规矩。如果你不打算买，绝对不要还价。可是实际上那个小贩并不是在公平交易。我对他说：“你从三千一下子降到两百，我怎么能相信你？现在我知道你的筷子是骨头的，不是象牙的。对不起。如果你一开始要价四百的话就不一样了。你从一开始就想占顾客的便宜，结果是搬起石头砸自己的脚。”

事情并没有结束。我看了所有的商品，就是没发现我想买的佛手。我正要离开，另外一个人拿着一双筷子出现了。“这是我的，不是那个人的。”实际上，这第二个人的筷子连骨头的都不是，是塑料的。

Authentic fakes

I never pay attention to fashion and brands. I wear what I feel comfortable and convenient. Decades ago, my 10-year-old Italian nephew asked me for jeans from Canada when I would go there. Upon seeing them, he exclaimed they were not Levis. "What does Levis mean?" I asked naively. Later, I was preparing to come to China when my Sichuan friend ordered jeans for her daughter. "You mean Levis, I guess?" "No, Benetton," she said.

Living in China I realize the impact the brand image has on people here. Once I bought a pair of sandals because I needed sandals. More Non-Chinese than Chinese told me, "Wow! You wear that? You have money!" I didn't know why they thought 150-yuan sandals – obviously fake – were for wealthy people. I had never heard that name (which I can't remember) before.

While visiting my family in Canada, we were talking about false-fraud-fake products in China. I assured them I would never buy imitations. As a writer, I don't accept that readers pirate my books and I would consider myself a thief if ever I buy counterfeits. A young relative said, "What about your purse?" "What's the problem with my purse?" I countered. "It's a Yves Saint-Laurent; do you mean you paid the full price?" "How can you think I bought a YSL? I bought it because of size, color, and price." She picked up the purse and pointed to the 3-cm steel YSL on the flap. Believe me or not, I had not noticed it till then.

When Hong Qiao Market (now known as the Pearl Market) used to sell forged watches (hum!), I happened to need a watch and went

正宗的假货

我从来不注意时尚和名牌。什么舒服方便我就穿什么。几十年前，我10岁的意大利外甥让我从加拿大给他带一条牛仔裤。看到我给他带的牛仔裤时，他大叫说那不是李维斯的。“李维斯是什么？”我天真地问道。后来，我去中国的时候，我的四川朋友让我给她女儿带牛仔裤。我问：“你是要李维斯的吗？”“不是，我要贝纳通牌，”她说。

住在中国，我逐渐认识到了名牌对人们的影响。有一次我需要拖鞋，就买了一双。有很多人，特别是外国人对我说：“哇！你穿这个啊？你真有钱！”我不知道150元一双，但显然是假名牌的拖鞋，对有钱人意味着什么。我以前从来没听说过那个牌子（现在我已记不清）。

我回加拿大探亲的时候，跟家人说起中国的假冒伪劣名牌产品。我跟他们说，我决不会买冒牌货。作为一个作家，我不会接受别人盗版我的书。如果我买盗版货，我会认为自己是个贼。亲戚中一个年青人说：“那你的钱包呢？”“我的钱包怎么了？”我问道。“那是伊夫圣罗兰牌。你敢说你是付全款买的吗？”“你怎么会认为我买了伊夫圣罗兰牌子？我买的时候看的就是大小、颜色和价格。”她拿起钱包，把上面一个3厘米见方的伊夫圣罗兰金属标牌指给我看。可是，我此前从来没有注意过那个牌子，信不信由你。

有一次，我正好需要一块手表，就去了红桥市场（现叫珍珠市场），因为那里手表的种类很多。我说我需要买块表，只是看时间而已。可是

there for the large choice they offered. What I wanted was a watch to see the time, I insisted. They had no Chinese brands, only Cartier, Citizen, Seiko, Rolex… Desperately, I finally bought a Gucci for which I paid 20 yuan, bargained down from 168 yuan. It still works after 14 years.

Recently, in a store at Zhongguancun, young vendors noticed my watch and asked me how much I paid. I joked: "20,000 yuan." While expecting a laugh, I got a "Oh!" full of admiration. I gave them the watch to examine, but that only ended up convincing them it was an authentic Gucci. "I want to sell it, I'm tired of it. What about 2,000 yuan?" I offered. "It's still too much for us." I then asked what Chinese merchants ask: "How much do you want to pay?" No one dared giving an answer. "Well, I will leave it for 200," I concluded. "Is it fake?" one finally asked.

Two years ago, a family member needed an inexpensive watch with a blue plastic wristband for a special occasion, something that has a little girl look," she said, adding "a local one, not a famous brand." Hong Qiao was the market for children's watches. Having refused several *mingpai* copies, I was leaving without buying when I saw a blue plastic one. 'Diesel, what a strange name for a watch', I thought. Wasn't diesel something that went into a gas tank?

The transaction went quickly; I offered 35 yuan and left with the watch. Again I had been naive, I discovered later.

As for DVDs, I never bought pirated ones. Knowingly, I mean. I used to get them from a shop for 15 yuan instead or five (at the end of the last century), and I had established a lending system to prevent my colleagues from buying fake ones. Once, the *China Daily* published a report on a dozen of DVD stores being closed by the police. I suggested the paper publish an article on how to distinguish false from genuine, but I'm still waiting for such information.

他们没有中国的牌子，只有卡地亚、西铁城、精工、劳力士什么的。最后，我没办法，只好买了一块古奇牌的。不过，我从 168 元还价到 20 元。14 年过去了，这块表还照走不误。

最近，在中关村一家商店里，有一些年轻的摊贩看见我的表，问我多少钱买的。我开玩笑说："两万。"我本来以为他们会笑我，可是他们却充满羡慕地"啊"了一声。我把表摘下来让他们看，他们却越看越相信那是真的。"我想卖掉，我戴烦了。两千块要不要？""2000 块也太贵，"他们说。然后我学着中国小贩的口气说："你们说给多少吧。"没有人敢回应。"给我两百，这表就是你们的了，"我最后说。终于一个人问道："这是假的吗？"

两年前，我的一个亲戚为了某个特殊的场合要买一块一般的手表，要求表带是塑料的、蓝色的。"女孩子戴的，"她说，"本地产的，不要名牌。"红桥市场卖各种儿童手表。小贩拿给我的都是各种假名牌，我一一拒绝了。我正要离开的时候，看见一块有蓝色塑料表带的。"Diesel"，真奇怪的手表牌子，那不是油箱里的柴油吗？我想。

买卖很顺利。我出价 35 元买下了这块表。后来我才发现，我还是太天真了。

至于光碟，我从来不买盗版的。我的意思是，不故意买盗版的。我都是从商店里买，花 15 元，而不是花 5 元（上个世纪末的价格）。我把看过的光碟借给同事，免得他们去买盗版的。《中国日报》有一次报道说，警察查封了一些 DVD 商店。我向《中国日报》建议：发表一篇如何区别真假光盘的文章。但是，直到现在我也没见到这方面的信息。

China, and the rest of the world

"OK, everyone squeeze in" was the title of a very interesting article published on *China Daily*, June 4, 2010. It shows the problems and challenges that the six volunteers astronauts who have been selected for Mars 500 Mission will face during 520 days: eating canned food, being allowed to shower once every 10 days, having only a 3 sq. m room to stay alone when the presence of others becomes unbearable, never having a view on the outside, never see one family member during one and a half years, etc.

The project was launched by a team of Russian scientists in cooperation with the European Space Agency. When recruitment started in 2007, one of the most serious criteria was "perfect fluency in Russian and English". Though Russian is the native language of three participants out of the six, English is a foreign language for all of them. The Chinese participant Wang Yue said before being "imprisoned" for 520 days that he planned to learn Russian during the experience. That means he was accepted with only one of the compulsory languages and that he can communicate with the others only in English.

As a "foreign expert" in China since 1991, what I found the most difficult – sometimes during my life here – was never having the possibility to speak freely Italian or French with other native speakers who would also be my best friends. On this point, not only Wang Yue but also the French and the Italian-Columbian members will be psychologically challenged.

The article also says that Wang Yue will suffer more pressure than the others because "he comes from a cultural background more

中国与世界

2010 年 6 月 4 日,《中国日报》刊载了一篇很有意思的文章，题目是《大家都挤进来吧》。文章是关于被选中参加火星 500 实验舱的六名志愿者在 520 天里所面临的问题和挑战。他们将吃罐头食品，每 10 天才能洗浴一次，受不了别人的时候，每个人可以独自享用只有 3 平方米的空间，无法欣赏外面的景色，一年半内无法跟家人见面。

这个项目是由俄国科学家与欧洲航天局共同发起的。2007 年开始招募志愿者的时候有很多严格的条件，其中之一是“能够讲流利的俄语和英语”。六名航天员中，有三名母语是俄语；对六个人来说英语是外语。在开始“囚禁”生活前中国人王跃说，他准备在这段时间里学习俄语。这说明他被接受的时候只会说一种所要求的语言，他只能用英语跟别人交流。

1991 年，我开始在中国当“外国专家”。我发现在这里最难的一件事是，想要和好朋友用意大利语或法语无拘无束地交谈几乎是不可能的事。就这一点来说，不仅仅是王跃，法国志愿者和意裔哥伦比亚志愿者也都会遇到同样的心理挑战。

文章还说，跟其他志愿者比起来，王跃将会面临更大的压力，因为“在文化背景上王跃与其他五个人之间的差距比其他五个人相互之间的差距

distinct than the other five." This kind of comment is present in all what I read in the web – all what is written by Chinese authors, I mean. Here again, Chinese divide the world in two: "we" Chinese, and "you" the rest of the world. One article says that Wang would encounter different habits in his daily life. Another one says that he would face a conflict between Chinese culture and Western culture, including Russian, French, Japanese and Columbian cultures.

I wonder how the Russians will react when the French will embrace and kiss his five colleagues every morning. Where will the Columbian take his 12 grapes to swallow on the 12 midnight strokes on Dec. 31, one for each month of the year? And when Wang Yue will kindly remember to wish Merry Christmas to his crew members on Dec. 25, the Russians will find it a little early as they celebrate Nativity on Jan. 7 only.

The Russians will miss their goulash, the Italian his cheese, the Chinese his *miantiao* and the French his croissant and coffee.

When will the Chinese understand that there is not one but several Western cultures? In the experimental module, there will be side by side five different cultures (as Diego Urbina is Italian and Columbian), and Wang Yue's Chinese culture is not more peculiar, more distinct or more specific than any one of the others.

More, Wang, aged 26, is the youngest of the team, the others ranging from 27 to 38 years old. Therefore he should have greater ability to adapt to situations.

The experience consists in studying the effect on human beings of loneliness, stress, fatigue, boredom that can become agitation, nervousness, aggressiveness, discouragement. Among the six are physician, surgeon, engineers, and none of them is advantaged or disadvantaged for his educational background, his life and work experience, or his culture. Parting with the family is "just as it is for any other person", said mission captain Sitev.

要大一些”。中国人写的这类评论我在网上也看到很多。这里又出现了中国人把世界一分为二的倾向：“我们”中国人，“你们”外国人。其中一篇文章说，王跃会在日常生活中看到很多不同的生活习惯。另外一篇文章说他会遇到中国文化和西方文化的冲突，这里所谓西方包括俄国、法国、日本和哥伦比亚。

我不知道，如果法国人每天早上拥抱亲吻他的五名同事，俄国人会怎么反应？ 12 月 31 日午夜 12 点，哥伦比亚人从哪里找代表 12 个月的 12 颗葡萄呢？如果王跃在 12 月 25 日向其他人祝贺圣诞，俄国人会觉得太早了点儿，因为他们只在每年 1 月 7 日庆祝圣诞节。

俄国人会怀念他们的古拉什牛肉汤，意大利人会怀念他的奶酪，中国人会怀念他的面条，法国人会怀念他的羊角面包和咖啡。

中国人什么时候才能懂得西方文化不止一种？在实验舱里，将有五种文化并存（迪亚哥－乌宾那有意大利和哥伦比亚双重国籍），王跃的中国文化并不比任何一个人的更为独特。

王跃是最年轻的，才 26 岁。其他成员的年龄从 27 岁到 38 岁不等，与他们相比，王应该更容易适应实验舱的生活环境。

这次实验要研究孤独、压力、疲劳和厌倦对人类的影响。这些问题可能导致情绪不稳、神经紧张、富有攻击性和失望沮丧。六名志愿者的职业有军医、外科大夫和工程师等。他们当中任何一个人的教育背景、生活背景、工作经验和文化背景既不优于也不次于其他人。实验项目的负责人希特夫说：“对任何人来说，同家人分离的感觉都是一样的。”

Capitalizing on wrong values

It's over a month that I'm thinking over and over about three recent phenomena which – for me – prove that Chinese values are not always the best ones.

First, at the end of January 2010, the Chinese mountain previously known as the "Southern Sky Column" in South China had been renamed, by the local government, "Avatar Hallelujah Mountain". The stunning mountains which inspired Avatar's floating peaks were modeled after the Huangshan Mountains of Anhui Province. But let apart romanticism, it seems that most of Cameron's movie was done in Los Angeles and New Zealand's studios.

Avatar earned more than US$80 million in China, and Zhangjiajie, a part of Wulingyuan National Park, will not miss an opportunity to capitalize on the movie's fame. The Zhangjiajie branch of CITS even launched a "Magical tour to Avatar-Pandora's floating mountain".

What is shocking is that fame is related to money. Have the Wulingyuan National Park of Hunan Province – listed as a UNESCO World Heritage Site – and the Yellow Mountains become more attractive since the movie was "inspired by them" in 2008? If the movie hadn't been a box office hit, would tourists flock to the spots now?

The second problem is that popularity in China is related to what is "foreign" more often than what it is worth. Featuring a Hong Kong-based hotel group called Shangri-La Hotels and Resorts, which is opening a hotel in Lhasa, the article's author was unable to escape mentioning that the group took its name from "Shangri-La", an area hidden within Tibet's peaks that is the setting in James Hilton's novel *Lost Horizon*.

生财无道

最近一个多月，我在反复思考三件事情，我觉得中国人的价值观并非总是最好的。

第一件事情是，2010 年 1 月，中国南方一座叫作“南天一柱”的山峰被当地政府改叫阿凡达－哈利路亚山了。电影《阿凡达》里面那些悬浮山的灵感来自于安徽黄山。可除了其中的浪漫色调，卡梅隆的电影大部分其实是在洛杉矶和新西兰的摄影棚里拍摄的。

阿凡达电影在中国赚了八千多万美元。因此，作为武陵源国家公园组成部分的张家界便不肯放过这个借电影之名分一杯羹的机会。国旅张家界分社甚至推出了一个“阿凡达——潘多拉神奇之旅”的项目。

令人吃惊的是，名声和钱连在了一起。2008 年，湖南的武陵源国家公园与安徽黄山都在联合国教科文组织世界遗产名录之列。难道就因为 2008 年《阿凡达》电影从中获得了灵感，这两个地方就更引人入胜了吗？如果该电影没有票房成功，游客现在还会蜂拥到这些景点去吗？

第二件事情是，在中国，一种东西不论价值如何，只要是跟外国沾边，便吃香起来。有一篇文章，作者在报道香港的香格里拉酒店集团在拉萨开分店时，忘不了提上一句，酒店的名称来自西藏群山中的一个隐秘所在，这个地方是詹姆士·希尔顿的小说《失落的地平线》所描述故事发生的地方。

If the novel had been written by a Chinese, the name Shangri-La (meaning "where all is perfect" or "Shambala" in Tibetan) would have remained unknown. Though this novel doesn't deserve the fame it had, in China it became famous because the author was a foreigner. Anytime the name Shangri-La is mentioned, for any reason, one may be sure that further in the sentence, James Hilton and *Lost Horizon* will be mentioned.

My third point is about an education process which I estimate wrong. Just because I love China doesn't mean I praise everything here.

Most Chinese believe that in western countries, anyone can enter university or college without an exam, and without fees. If countries such as Canada don't have a national entrance exam, it's because admission is based on a series of credits obtained through middle and high school marks. These marks are the total of regular tests, end of term exams, and creative works. The students are used to this. The final high school exams only account for a part of all that is considered for entrance, a kind of cherry on top of the cake. It would be impossible for an unprepared student to pass the final exam if he or she had not made successful steps all the way long before.

In such a system, students are encouraged to relax the last day before exams, because the game is over. They would watch TV, surf the web, have a chat with friends or read a book.

During the last exam period in China, Shanxi Linxian County ordered the Internet cafés to close in an effort to help students prepare for their exams. First, such order deprived the internet café owners of their income. Second, it deprived the customers of their right to the service. Third, the resolution sounded like a joke in a country where children are conditioned to national college entrance exam from birth.

How would a Chinese student dare going to an Internet café in the period his or her mother takes off work to cook good meals for her beloved treasure? If they dare, then the education process has failed. To educate a child is to develop his ability to manage his life, handle crisis, take responsibilities and make decisions.

假如这本小说是一个中国人写的，香格里拉（其意思是“完美之地”，藏语是“香巴拉”）大概就会湮没无闻。虽然这本小说本身不值得大加赞誉，在中国却成了名著，因为是一个外国人写的。每次提到香格里拉这个词，不管是出于什么原因，你都会在随后的文字中看到詹姆士·希尔顿的名字和他所写的《失落的地平线》。

我要说的第三件事与教育有关。我认为中国人在这个问题上的认识是错误的。虽然我热爱中国，但是这并不意味着我要赞美这里的一切。

大部分中国人相信，在西方国家，不需要考试，也不用花钱，任何人都能上大学或学院。加拿大的确没有全国性的高考，可大学录取必须以初中和高中取得的一系列学分为基础。这些成绩包括平常的考试、期末考试和学生的创造性作业。加拿大的中学生们习惯了这种制度。高中最后的考试只是大学录取所要参考的成绩的一部分，好比是蛋糕上装饰的几颗樱桃。如果一个学生在此前的学习中没有打下成功的基础，就不可能通过最后的考试的。

基于这种体制，考试之前，一般都鼓励学生放松，因为学习任务至此已经完成了。他们可以看电视、上网、跟朋友聊天，或者浏览闲书。

然而，上次中国高考的时候，山西林县却下令关闭网吧，说是要帮助学生准备考试。我认为，这种禁令首先让网吧业主失去了收入，其次剥夺了顾客享用网吧服务的权利。另外，在一个孩子们生来就被训练应对高考的国度里，这种禁令简直是个笑话。

当一个母亲为了给自己的孩子做可口的饭菜而放下工作的时候，哪个孩子胆敢去网吧呢？如果他们真敢去，那么教育就算失败了。教育孩子就是要培养他们管理生活、处理危机、承担责任、作出决策的能力。

Learning Chinese, such an exploit!

The first question Chinese persons ask to their non-Chinese counterparts is… In fact, they don't ask a question but expect you to confirm their statement: "Learning Chinese is very difficult."

What makes Chinese hard for a learner whose native language uses Latin alphabet? Only the Chinese characters, or sinogrammes. In this case, a learner of Cyrillic, Arabic, Tibetan or Hindi faces the same challenge. Chinese is even easier because its *pinyin* helps a lot. But if the newcomer is satisfied, at least at the beginning, with spoken Chinese, and doesn't wish to read and write the sinogrammes, things become even simpler.

The more languages one knows, the easier it is to acquire a new one. If a learner masters English, Chinese grammar will then appear not only similar, but even less complicated than English, except for the measure words which categorize nouns. But don't English speakers also say "a cup" of tea, "a glass" of wine, "a slice" of bread?

A relative of mine is learning Chinese by herself. I made a list of the mainly used measure words with one or two examples for her to memorize. For instance, I told her: "When you order a roast duck, you say '*Yizhi kaoya*', as a duck is a bird."

Several days later she asked me why cats used the same particle as birds in Chinese. "Is it because cats eat birds?"

"No, cat is a feline."

"So, I must use *zhi* for lion and tiger too, right?"

"Well… not exactly. Tiger requires *zhi*, but lion wants a *tou* (head)."

"Didn't you say *tou* was for farm animals such as cow, sheep, pig, horse and donkey?"

中文好难学

中国人见到非中国人问的第一个问题就是……其实也不是问题，他们就是想让你证实一下他们的论断，那就是“学中文很难。”

一个母语使用拉丁字母的人学中文，什么东西显得那么难学呢？那就是汉字。其实，学斯拉夫语，学阿拉伯语，学藏语或者印第语的都面临着同样的挑战。中文似乎更容易一些，因为拼音帮了很大的忙。如果初学者只想学习汉语口语，而不打算掌握读写，那就更简单了。

一个人懂的语言越多，学习一种新语言就越容易。对掌握了英语的人来说，除了量词以外，中文语法不但类似英语，而且更简单。况且，英文中不是也有“a cup” of tea（一杯茶）,“a glass” of wine（一杯酒),“a slice” of bread（一片面包）吗？

我的一个亲戚在自学中文。我给她做了一个常用量词表，附上一两个例子，供她记忆。比如，我告诉她：“如果你要买烤鸭，你就说‘一只烤鸭’，因为鸭属于鸟类。”

几天后她问我为什么猫跟鸟用一样的量词,“是不是因为猫吃鸟啊？”

“不是，猫是猫科动物。”

“那我也应该用‘只’说狮子和老虎，对吗？”

“嗯，不尽然。说老虎用‘只’，说狮子用‘头’”。

“你不是说‘头’是用于说牲畜吗，比如牛、羊、马和驴？”

"Yes, but not exclusively and not all of them. The horse doesn't share its fellow donkey's bed and requires *pi*. And the pig is so greedy that it has two measure words: *tou* or *kou* (mouth)."

"Gosh, I will never learn! What about the dog?"

I felt a little embarrassed to tell her that dog requires *tiao* (length) as it belongs to the category of long things, such as pants and skirts, noodles, snake and fish.

"I got it!" she said, adding to the list cigarette and pencil.

"Pencil and cigarette... no. They need *gen*. Also hair, match, and rope, you see?"

"What I see is that the basic concept of the theory is not logical." I didn't dare to protest, as this was exactly my own conclusion 20 years ago when I was groping in the dark tunnel of learning Chinese by myself. But I tried to encourage and help her find certain standards.

"Look, what is common between a table, a bed, a postage stamp and a sheet of paper?"

"They are all flat. And all quadrangular."

"You are absolutely right. So they share the same measure word: *zhang*."

At that point she couldn't but laugh. I asked why.

"I think I can add *zhang* before my brother-in-law's name; he too is square and flat," she said.

After this diversion, she added:

"Wait a minute, just before I came here, I checked this measure word in the dictionary, and I read it was used to categorize mouth, bow, and fishing net! Flat and square, hey? Are we talking about the same 张? The one that is also a family name?"

"Exact."

"Meh! I better not try to understand and just learn as it is."

"Don't you find this fun to learn? Measure words are what I liked best when I started studying Chinese. They make Chinese language special! All the rest is so predictable."

“对，不过不是仅用于牲畜，而且不是用于所有牲畜的。马跟驴就不一样，得用‘匹’。猪的胃口很大，需要两个量词，‘头’和‘口’。”

“天哪！这叫我怎么学啊？那说狗怎么办呢？”

我很不好意思地告诉她说狗要用“条”，因为狗属于长条类的东西，比如裤子、裙子、面条、蛇和鱼。

“我懂了！”她说，随即自己推广到香烟和铅笔。

“香烟和铅笔？不不不！它们得用‘根’。头发、火柴和绳子也都用‘根’，懂了吗？”

“我看这个理论一点也不合乎逻辑，”她说。我未敢反驳她，因为20年前我在昏暗的中文隧道中摸索的时候，也曾得出过同样的结论。但我还是努力鼓励她，帮助她找到一些规律性的东西。

“想想看，桌子、床、邮票和纸有什么共同点？”

“都是平的、四方型的。”

“太对了，所以他们都用一个量词‘张’。”

听我这么一说她忍不住笑了。我问她笑什么。

“我想我可以把这个‘张’放在我妹夫的名字前头，因为他也是又方又平的。”

然后言归正传，她又说：“我来这里以前，刚刚在字典里查了这个量词。字典里说它放在嘴、弓箭和鱼网之前。你不是说又平又方吗？我们是不是在说同一个‘张’字啊？就是那个姓张的‘张’？”

“当然啦！”

“咳，我干脆甭捉摸了，照着用就是了。”

“你不觉得学这个很好玩吗？我刚学中文的时候，量词是我最喜欢的。中文之为中文就在于量词！除了量词，别的都是可以预料得到的。”

The pajama dilemma

Once, a worker rang my doorbell at 8:10 am to repair the toilet. "I was expecting you early," I said, "but not so early." What I added in my imperfect Chinese – "I have not yet put my clothes on" – sounded like I was naked. In fact, shocked into my sense of propriety, I had quickly slipped a robe over my nightgown before opening the door. Seeing the man staring at me wide-eyes, I realized that I should have said: "I have not yet changed my sleeping clothes for my day clothes". But I didn't make any correction. We were both embarrassed enough.

The last half-year before Shanghai World Expo began, much has been said and written about Shanghai people, for whom wearing pajamas has become fashionable everywhere and anytime. I heard that there was a public campaign calling on people not to wear pajamas outside their house. Has it succeeded? I don't know as I have not visited Shanghai since.

When I came to China two decades ago, I tried to buy pajamas at the Silk Market for relatives and friends abroad. Vendors had no idea what a pajama was as the Chinese were used to sleeping in their underwear. Maybe it is foreigners' demand that has created a market for pajamas.

Now, many Chinese, both urban and rural, around the country, buy pajamas not as sleepwear but for their comfort. A grandmother wearing a Mickey Mouse patterned pajama or an old man with Teddy bears on his can be seen easily, as they go to the market and to the park after dinner; some even venture to cinemas and the subway,

睡衣困境

一天，一个工人早上八点十分来按门铃，给我修理厕所。“我知道你会早来，可是没想到这么早，”我用不太熟练的中文说，“我还没有穿衣服。”听起来好像我光着身子一样。实际上，修理工的到来让我大吃一惊，为了体面，开门之前我匆匆忙忙地在睡衣外面又穿了件长袍。开门之后，那个男子吃惊地看着我。我意识到我应该说“我还没有换上白天穿的衣服”，而不是“我还没有穿衣服”，但是我没有纠正我自己。我们都觉得很不好意思。

上海世博会开幕前半年，广播里、报纸上到处有关于上海人的说法，说他们现在很流行穿睡衣，不分场合和时间。我还听说，有人发起一个运动，号召大家不要在家以外的地方穿睡衣。这个运动是否奏效，我不得而知，因为我后来没有去过上海。

20 年前刚来中国时，我去北京秀水市场给国外的亲戚朋友买睡衣。卖服装的不知道什么是睡衣，因为中国人习惯于穿内衣内裤睡觉。也许是因为外国人的需求才推动了睡衣市场的发展。

现在很多中国人，全国各地都有，为了舒适而不是为了睡觉买睡衣。在街头，很容易看到一个老太太穿着米老鼠图案的睡衣，或者一个老头穿着泰迪熊图案的睡衣。他们或者去市场买菜，或者晚饭后去公园遛弯。

while for us, Westerners, a pajama is linked to intimacy. This is what makes a "pajama party" something unusual.

I have a friend in Beijing who is in her 30s and has a 1-year-old daughter. Today's young mothers can't make it alone with a child, and most of them hire a maid. Every time I visit my friend, the maid, who lives with the family, is in her pajamas. I find it weird, but I tell myself "she is at home" after all.

My friend Ann is very elegant in her brand-name dresses, but I have seen even her in pajamas. Ann does not cook. It is her husband who usually does, but as he leaves on business trips often, the couple asked Ann's father to come from Shanghai and take charge of the kitchen. I have known the man since the 1990s and always thought he was not only handsome but good-mannered too.

On my last visit, I could not believe my eyes: when the grandfather opened the door, with the baby in his arms, he was wearing cotton underwear. I had a chance to discover he was also very sexy! Looking away, I apologized as if I had done something wrong.

Had he come to the door expecting someone else? Not at all! I was embarrassed, but he was not. "Come in! Have a seat! Ann will be here in a moment," he invited, and instead of running directly into his bedroom, he also sat and started a conversation. Then appeared my friend – in her new dress, and well made-up.

If you insist on knowing my opinion, I would say one would not wear plastic sandals to a dinner, nor the most attractive bathing suit to go to the bank. It's only a matter of convenience and taste.

有的甚至这副打扮去看电影或者坐地铁。对于我们西方人来说，睡衣意味着亲密。这就是为什么所谓的“睡衣聚会”不同寻常。

我有个北京朋友，三十来岁，有个一岁的女儿。今天的年轻母亲们一个人带孩子很难，大部分都雇保姆。我每次去我这个朋友家的时候，她家的住家保姆都是穿着睡衣。我觉得很奇怪，但是我告诉自己：“毕竟她这还是在屋里。”

我有个朋友叫安，穿名牌衣服时很雅气，但我也见过她穿睡衣的时候。安在家里不做饭，一般都是丈夫做。丈夫出差的时候，他们就请安的爸爸从上海过来做饭。我从 20 世纪 90 年代起就认识她爸爸了。我觉得她爸爸不但人长得英俊，而且举止也很讲究。

上一次去她家的时候，我简直不敢相信自己的眼睛：安的爸爸抱着小孩开门的时候，穿的是棉布内衣，因而我有机会发现他还很性感！我把眼睛挪开，赶紧道歉，好像是我做错了什么。

他是不是在等别人呢？根本不是！我觉得不好意思，他却和没事儿人一样。“请进！请坐！安一会儿就回来。”他没有马上跑回他的卧室，而是坐下来，开始跟我聊天。这时候我的朋友回来了，穿着一身新衣服，体体面面。

如果你要问我的意见，我觉得谁都不应该穿塑料拖鞋外出吃饭，也不应该穿吸引眼球的泳装去银行。这本是一个方便与品位需要兼顾的问题。

South Korea was so different!

Recently I visited South Korea. First of all, I must confess I had an absolutely wrong idea of this country as I thought it was completely Americanized. So, I didn't even make the effort of learning "Hello," "Please" and "Thank you" in Korean before going.

The youths all study English but, like in China, can hardly speak it. When buying things, hands are the most useful instrument. Public signs (except commercial advertisement) are written in Korean, English and Chinese, and sometimes Japanese also. But some English signs are different from the English signs used in China; for instance, "Way out" is always used instead of "Exit". Street names are indicated in Latin alphabet, but the spelling is not standard and I was never sure whether Kyong, Jeong, Geyong were different names or the same.

Not only South Korea was different from the one in my imagination, but its historical culture, its art concepts, its way of living, and the way people consider non-Koreans and interact with them immersed me in a word totally different from China.

My first impression was an olfactory one: From the moment I got out of the airport, I smelled "wood", just to discover that the country is totally green. Mountains and hills, making 70 percent of the area, are visible everywhere and are all covered with forests and woods. In the fields are rice paddies or vegetables. On both sides of the highways are trees, and on both sides of the city streets and alleys, are potted green plants, flowers, or red chillies.

In a way to allow cars to circulate in narrow alleys, people use plastic pots. These pots are vertically cut in two parts, and each part has a flat back. What an ingenious space saver!

韩国如此不同

最近，我访问了韩国。首先，我要坦白一下：我过去以为韩国完全美国化了，所以我出发之前，根本没有想到要学几句韩国话，比如“你好”“请”“谢谢”等。但是事实并非如我所料。

在韩国，年轻人都学英语，但是像在中国一样，几乎说不了什么英语。我在韩国购物的时候，手势是最好的工具。公共招牌（除了商业广告以外）是用韩文、英文和中文写的，有的时候也有日文。但有的地方的英语跟中国的不一样。比如，在韩国，他们用“Way Out”表示“出口”，而不是用“Exit”。街道的名称是用拉丁字母拼写的，但是拼写并没有统一的标准。我总是搞不清楚“Kyon”“Jeong”“Geyong”是同一个名字，还是不同的名字。

韩国不但跟我想象的不同，其历史文化、艺术观念、生活方式，对外国人的认知，与外国人交往的方式，都让我看到一个完全不同于中国的世界。

味觉是我的第一个印象。我一出机场，就闻到了“树木”的味道。这个国家完全是绿色的。高山丘陵占全国的百分之七十，但到处都是郁郁葱葱的。田野里是稻田和菜地。公路两边树木成荫，城市里街道的两旁是一盆盆的花草和红辣椒。

It was raining when I arrived, what could amplify the wood odor on streets and in parks, but I noticed that houses, museums, and commercial buildings also smelled of wood, as Koreans use a lot of wood in building and decoration.

My second impression was that Koreans were disciplined drivers and pedestrians. Coming from China, it was not difficult noticing the difference. The street light system is very well organized. I didn't see any pedestrian crossing a street on red light or where there were no white lines. The lines are large and they go in two directions, allowing a crowd to cross in one or the other direction without bumping other pedestrians. Following the rules, I never had to check whether a car or a bicycle would hit me. It was good to feel safe!

I had met a Korean couple on my flight from Beijing, and they invited me to Chungju, in the center of the country. Staying in a real family for three days, I had a chance to learn about Korean customs and culture. For example, it's compulsory to take off your shoes not only in a house but in temples, some boutiques, and even in traditional style restaurants where people sit on the floor around a square low table. I also learned how they make the omnipresent *kimchi* (picked vegetables), and the soya sauce, in huge quantity that they keep for two to three years. Some restaurants boast having 10-year-old *da jiang*.

The food is mostly steamed, boiled, or roasted; not fried. Though Koreans are fond of coffee – and it's not because it is fashionable –, they seldom take some at breakfast. But all kinds of coffee shops are full of customers. One can even have a jelly-coffee!

When I was by myself, I tried a different dish everyday at restaurant. The last day I asked for noodles with an egg on top, and showed the picture on the wall. But as I don't like cold noodles (a Korean specialty), I showed the blue and the pink buttons of the water machine to the waitress, saying and gesturing "No" for the cold-blue and "Yes" for the warm-pink. She seemed having got my thought: she

为了让车辆在狭窄的街巷中行驶，人们将塑料花盆一分为二，每个花盆都是半圆的，多么聪明的设计！

我到达的时候正在下雨。这让街头和公园的树木的味道更为明显。但是我注意到房屋、博物馆和商业建筑也散发着木头的味道，因为韩国人在建筑和装饰上也大量使用木头。

我对韩国的第二个印象是，韩国人开车走路都很守规矩。我是从中国来到这里的，自然注意到了这种差别。交通信号灯的组织功能得到很好发挥。红灯亮的时候，或者没有白线的地方，没有人过马路。人行横道很宽，而且是双向设计，可以让很多人过马路而不致互相冲撞。在这样的交通规则下，我不用担心自己会被汽车或者自行车撞到。能安全过马路的感觉太好了！

在去韩国的飞机上，我遇到一对韩国夫妇。他们请我到韩国中部的忠州市访问。在一个韩国人家里住了三天，我得到了解韩国的风俗习惯和文化的机会。在韩国，不但进家门要脱鞋，而且进庙宇、小店以及席地而坐围桌而食的传统餐馆，也要脱鞋。我也了解了有名的泡菜和大酱的做法。他们大量制作，可以保存两三年。有的餐馆自诩存有 10 年之久的大酱。

韩国饭主要是蒸、煮和烤制的，很少炸。韩国人也喜欢咖啡，而且并非为了赶时髦，可他们也很少在吃早饭的时候喝咖啡。然而，街头的咖啡馆总是宾客盈门，你甚至可以点一个咖啡冻。

我独自一个人的时候，总是喜欢每天在餐馆点一个不同的菜式。最

brought me – with a large smile – a big glass of hot water to drink, and my noodles in a chilled broth.

With my host, Chinese was our common language. Once, while visiting a historical site, there was a word I knew only in English, and his English knowledge didn't include that word. So he called his son (who studies in China). He unfolded his handkerchief to cover his cell phone, and explained to me that the use of cell phone was forbidden in public places, on bus and subway, and in parks. There is no music in stations, stores, and taxis. People talk in low voice, on a sweet tone. Just like a song! You can imagine how I found the voice volume striking on my return to Beijing!

In fact, his wife explained to me later that using a cell phone in public was not forbidden by law, but such behavior was not polite, then people just didn't do it.

Smoking is forbidden in several "green zones" even in the open air. I was told that 50 percent of the Koreans smoke, but in fact, I was disturbed by a cigarette smell only three times in two weeks.

Museums are often free, or the admission price is very reasonable. Seoul National Museum is huge, as huge as History. I concentrated on the Unified Shilla Period. As summer holidays were still lasting, parents with children were visiting. Among foreign and local tourists, Chinese families were the most numerous, but their interests and behavior were very different. Would you hear visitors laughing loudly or shouting, you unfortunately knew where they were from.

Catholic and protestant churches can be seen everywhere, but Buddhism is the major religion. However, temples and imperial palaces are much smaller than those in China, and their decoration is modest in comparison. I was following a group of Chinese tourists when I heard the guide saying that there was no one building over 30 years old, that all had been destroyed by the Japanese hundreds of times, and rebuilt recently.

后一天，我要一份面条，上面放一个鸡蛋。我把墙上的照片指给他们看。我不喜欢冷面（韩国特色），我通过一个饮水机的红、蓝按钮示意女招待，指着蓝色按钮说"不要"，指着红色按钮说"要"。她似乎懂得了我的意思，笑眯眯地给我送来了一大杯热水，还有一碗冷面！

我也跟我的主人用中文交流。有一次，我们参观一个古迹的时候，我只知道一个词的英文，而他的英文词汇里却没有那个词。于是他打电话向在中国上学的儿子求助。他打开手绢盖住手机，并对我说，在巴士、地铁和公园等公共场所禁止打手机。在车站、商店和出租车里没有音乐。人们讲话都压低嗓门，但声音甜美如同歌唱。你可以想象，我回到北京时，面对北京街头的嘈杂我又是什么感觉。

后来，这家主人的太太告诉我，其实并无法律规定禁止在公共场所使用手机，但是这样做有违礼貌，所以大家都不用手机。

有些"绿色区域"是禁止吸烟的，即便是露天场所也不例外。我听说，50% 的韩国人吸烟，但两周的时间里只有三次我受到烟味骚扰。

韩国的博物馆不是免费的就是门票非常合理。首尔国家博物馆很大，像历史本身一样悠久而宏大。我主要参观了有关新罗时期的部分。暑假还没有结束，家长们带着孩子在参观。在外国游客和本地游客中，中国家庭最多，可是他们的兴趣和行为非常不同。如果你听见游客大声喊叫说笑，你就很不幸地知道他们是从哪里来的。

天主教堂和基督教堂随处可见，但是佛教是韩国的主要宗教。不过，韩国的庙宇和宫殿比中国的小得多，装饰也比中国的简朴。我跟着一群中国游客，导游介绍说，那里没有一个建筑的历史超过 30 年，且多次遭到日本人破坏，现存的都是新近重建的。

From that guide I learned two other interesting things: Indian dragons have six claws at each foot, Chinese ones have five, Korean, four, and Japanese, three. I had never paid attention to that. The other information was that only 11 of the 12 Zodiacal animals were represented in the palace we were visiting. The Dog was missing, "because it was considered dirty," said the guide. "Dog meat was eaten by the poor only."

In fact I was unable to find dog meat on menus. It is served only in special restaurants, I was told, and nowadays very few Koreans still eat it.

Public buses are fast and comfortable. Once I was sitting on the left side, and on the right side was an early-20-year-old girl, alone. She ate some kind of junk food. Once the bag was empty, she crumpled it, and put it in the net pocket in front of her. Then she meticulously wiped each finger on the velvet covered seat. When we were about to get off, I spoke to her in Chinese. Surprised, she asked me how I knew she was Chinese. I turned my wide open eyes to the greasy bag. She blushed. I suggested, with a smile: "Don't let people think Chinese are uncivilized, would you?"

I spent half of my time in the southeast – Busan, Gyeongku – the ancient capital of Shilla Dynasty, the sea, the countryside. I noticed that, just like in Canada, to be a farmer is not belonging to a social class but doing "that" work instead of another. Farmers have the same houses, same cars, same services and same education as urban citizens.

I also realized that adobe houses, with dirt floor, no running water inside and no toilets – houses that in China are still inhabited mostly in the south and by ethnic minorities – belong to the past in South Korea and are visited as history museum.

Development started under the dictatorial rule of President Park Chung-hee at about the same time the Reform and Opening policy started in China, but the results seemed to me – in what I could see – far well-distributed, probably due to the smaller territory and population of the country.

从那个导游那里，我还知道了另外两件有趣的事：印度的龙爪有六趾，中国的是五趾，韩国的是四趾，日本的是三趾。我从来没有留心过这个。另外一件事是，在我们参观的宫殿里，十二生肖却只有十一个动物，其中没有狗。导游说："韩国人认为狗很脏，只有穷人才吃狗肉。"

实际上，我在菜单中没有发现狗肉，只有在专门的餐馆中才有。现在很少有韩国人吃狗肉了。

韩国的公交车又快又舒服。有一次我坐在左边，右边是一个20出头的女孩。她正独自吃某种垃圾食品，吃完以后，她把食品袋子揉成一团，放在她前边的网兜里，然后用绒面的椅罩把十个手指仔细地擦干净。我们快下车的时候，我用中文对她讲话。她大吃一惊，问我怎么知道她是中国人。我睁大了眼睛，盯着那个油渍渍的食品袋。她脸红了。我笑着对她说："别让人觉得中国人很不文明，好吗？"

我旅程的一半时间花在了东南部——釜山和庆州（新罗的古都）的海岸和乡村。我注意到，就像在加拿大一样，务农不属于某个社会阶层，只是一种职业。农民和城里人一样，享有住房、汽车、服务和教育。

我也注意到，类似中国南方少数民族居住的那种只有泥土地面、没有自来水和厕所的砖坯房，在韩国已经成为历史，只作为博物馆供人参观。

韩国的经济发展开始于朴正熙的独裁统治时期，与中国实施改革开放的时间大致相当。在我看来，经济发展在韩国是非常均衡的，这或许是由于这个国家人口少、地域小的缘故。

Finally, I think that South Koreans know how to preserve their culture: in language, cuisine, housing architecture, social customs, and even in clothing I could find ethnic choice of colors and style. Even Buddhist nuns and monks wear Korean style attire. Generally speaking, South Korea is far less globalized, or Americanized, than China.

最后，我要说的是，韩国人知道怎样传承自己的语言、饮食、民居建筑和社会风俗文化。在服饰上，我也能看到他们民族的色彩和风格，就连尼姑、和尚都穿着韩式的僧服。总的来说,比起中国来,韩国全球化，或者说是美国化的程度要小得多。

To be late without losing face

The transportation went unexpectedly smoothly and I arrived at the meeting point half an hour before time. I kept my eyes on the restaurant door. Several customers entered, but not my friend. At 6 pm, she sent me a text message: "Urgent work to finish. Will be 20 min. late."

I had forgotten to take a book, so I spent time reflecting over my experiences about being late in China.

On my first visit in 1985, punctuality was deeply rooted in the Chinese morality. There were no traffic jams, and the expression "*du che*" (traffic jam) was unheard of.

Our tour guide told us that the bus would leave at 8:00 the next morning. But at 8:02, one person was still missing. The guide panicked: "Something must have happened? This is impossible! Maybe he overslept?" And she asked the reception desk to send someone to the absentee's room for a check.

As a teacher, in Canada, I always insisted on punctuality. I would open the classroom door to a late student for the first breach, and the second, but not the third. He or she would have to remain in the corridor and catch up at the end of the day when the others leave.

In one particular group of students, however, I had a bunch of guys who never cured their fault, including my son, who was born one week later than expected and never made up.

But as an Italian, I was used to the disregard of time anywhere and everywhere. During a summer vacation in Italy, we had an appointment at 7:30 pm with a notary. He arrived at 8:15. As we were old friends and had not seen each other for long, we chatted for a while. At 9:45, he said: "Too late to talk business; let's go to the bar."

迟到却没丢面子

交通顺利，我提前半个小时到达会面地点。在餐馆，眼睛紧盯着门口。几个顾客进来，但是没有我的朋友。6 点钟，她发来一个短信：“手头活儿紧，晚到 20 分钟。”

我忘了随身带本书来，等待中我回味起我在中国曾经的迟到经历。

1985 年初到中国，准时的概念深深扎根于中国人的行为准则中。当时，没有交通拥挤，“堵车”一词几乎是闻所未闻。

一次，导游告诉我们，次日 8 点巴士出发。8 点零 2 分，尚有一人未到。导游很着急：“一定出问题了！这简直不可能！他睡过头了吗？”她让前台服务员到迟到者的房间察看。

我在加拿大教书的时候，特别强调准时。学生一次迟到，或者两次迟到，我都会给他开门。但是事不过三，如若再迟到，学生就得留在走廊内，放学后补课。

可是，有一些学生总是屡教不改，其中也包括我的儿子。他是在预产期之后一个星期才出生的，从此永远迟到。

我是意大利血统，因此对各个地方不遵守时间的习惯已然适应。有一年在意大利过暑假，我们跟一个公证员约定在晚上 7：30 见面，他 8：15 才来。我们是老朋友，很久没见面了，所以我们聊起天来。到了 9：45，他说：“今天太晚了，事情办不成了，我们去喝酒吧。”

During the six years I worked with CCTV, I made a Chinese friend whom I often saw at lunch time or after work. We used to meet in the subway station nearby. He was always late by 10-20 minutes. To my question "You were busy?" he would surprisingly answer "No." Once, I asked him to check the clock in their office, thinking it must be wrong. It dawned on me later that this man was simply late-by-nature.

The last years of my work with Beijing Review, I had moved to Shunyi District near the Capital Airport. Though my schedule was quite flexible, I contracted a taxi to drive me to Dongzhimen subway station every morning, so I could reach my office at a decent time.

In March 2005, I was granted the permanent residence in China. The ceremony was planned for 9 am at the Public Security Bureau on the 2nd Ring Road.

I told my driver I had to get there by 8:40 the next morning. "No problem," he replied. But the next morning, he thought he had time to take someone to the airport before picking me up. He miscalculated, and I desperately waited for him. Then, to rub salt into my wounds, he needed to stop at the gas station.

Finally, I entered the room at 9:07 – the last guest to arrive. And here is the point: Instead of starting the meeting immediately, the organizers let 10 more minutes run – surreptitiously – in a way to make me at ease and cover my offence to politeness. In a word, they didn't make me lose face, and I will never forget their tactful kindness.

在中国央视工作的六年里，我认识了一个中国朋友。我们常常一起吃午饭或者下班后聚一聚，我们一般都是在附近的地铁站碰头。他总是迟到十到二十分钟。我问他："你忙吗？"他总是说："不忙。"有一次我让他检查一下办公室的钟，我想那个钟可能有问题。后来我才知道，迟到是他的"天性"。

在《北京周报》工作的最后几年里，我搬到了首都机场附近的顺义区。虽然我的工作时间是灵活的，我还是包了一辆出租，每天早上送我到东直门地铁站，这样就算我晚到，也不会晚得太离谱。

2005 年 3 月，我获得了中国的永久居民身份。外国人永久居民证的发放仪式定于 9 点在二环路的公安局举行。

头一天，我告诉司机次日我需要 8 点 40 分到达那里。"没问题，"他说。但是第二天早晨，他觉得他可以先送人到机场再接我也不迟。可是他的算盘打错了。我满怀焦虑地等着他，更糟心的是，他还得去加油。

结果，9 点 07 分我才到达现场，是最后一个到达的。可是我在这里要说的是，仪式的组织人员没有马上宣布开始，而是不动声色地推迟了 10 分钟，冲淡了我的尴尬，冲淡了我不礼貌的迟到可能造成的影响。他们没有让我丢脸，我也永远忘不了他们机智的善意。

Those who deserve it

Remarkable people are often unknown. And forgotten.

During my 20 years in China, I got to know many ordinary Chinese who were extraordinary. As the second Monday of October is Thanksgiving in my native country, Canada, I take this special occasion to commemorate some of those who brought me light along my way.

In 1989, I fell seriously ill in Beijing and was brought unconscious to my dormitory. A teacher bought some medicine for me, explained to me how to take it, and cycled home in a hurry. Twenty minutes later, he came back and begged me not to tell anyone that he had forgotten to give me the change: 3 *mao* (0.30 yuan). I knew he was sincere; I would surely not sully his reputation.

In 2001, on a request from her uncle, I hosted an 18 year-old girl from Inner Mongolia autonomous region. Upon her arrival, Tuoya opened the faucet to wash her hands. The water pressure was high and she immediately reduced the jet until only a trickle of water came out. She said: "We must save water!"

In Inner Mongolia, former lush grasslands have been reduced to deserts due to growing population and over-grazing. I thought I was aware of environmental issues, but I learned from her that I could save even more water.

Last year, I heard that Tuoya had become a taxi driver in HulunBuir. Strange for a girl who was car sick. One night, she didn't go home. The next day she was found killed in her car. She was 24.

那些值得尊重的人

优秀的人常常是无名英雄，而且也会被遗忘。

在中国二十多年，我遇到过很多非同寻常的普通人。每年十月第二个星期一是我的国家加拿大的感恩节，我不由得回忆起那些给我生活带来过光明的人。

1989 年，我在北京得了病，昏迷不醒，被人抬回宿舍。一个老师给我买了些药，告诉我怎么吃药后就赶紧骑车回家了。20 分钟后，他又回来了，说少找了我三毛钱，他还嘱咐我千万别告诉别人。我知道他是个诚实人，当然不会玷污他的声誉。

2001 年，应她叔叔的请求，我让一个 18 岁的内蒙古女孩托娅在家住了一段时间。到家后，她打开水龙头洗手。水压很高，她马上关小了笼头，让水流变得很细。她说：“我们要节约用水！”

在内蒙古，由于人口增长和过度放牧，有的地方绿色的草场已经变成了荒漠。我觉得自己对环境问题很有认识，可我从她那里学到了如何做到更节约。

去年，我听说托娅在呼伦贝尔当了出租司机。她过去是晕车的，居然开起了出租。有一天晚上，她没能回家。第二天，有人发现她已经在车里遇害了，当时她才 24 岁。

In 2003, my friend and I found a private driver named Zhang Jun in Qinghai province. He offered such a low price that we thought it was "per person". He brought us not only to the home of the late 10th Panchen Lama and the "Celestial Lake", but to a water spring hidden in the mountain, a century-old village with refined wooden sculptures that was far from our way, and the Wendusi Temple where we met his friend, a lama.

The perfect driver was very considerate. After his service was over, he unexpectedly picked us up at the hotel to help us reach our next destination, refusing any extra payment.

In 2005, the day I was suffering the deepest pain ever due to some personal issues, a friend called me from Shanghai ."If I go to Beijing tomorrow, will you be there?" I thought he was only trying to comfort me, but he showed up the very next day.

"I felt you needed to talk, so, here I am!" he said. In fact, I needed nothing other than an ear to confide to.

In 2007, I retired from work. Though I'm allowed to remain in China, as a foreigner, I don't enjoy any privilege such as pension or health insurance.

A former student of mine who lives in Hangzhou wrote: "My wife and I both agree that you come to live with us as long as you wish. Everyday you can go to the West Lake to read and write. You will have nothing to do, nothing to pay." I will not take advantage of the offer, but I shall always remember a remarkable display of "filial" love and respect.

During my years in the country, I have also been a victim of thefts; I have been used without knowing as a corruption instrument; I have been asked to conceal obvious fraud I had witnessed. But I prefer to remember those who deserve to be honored.

2003 年在青海，我和朋友雇到一个个体司机。他开价很低，我们还以为是按人头收费。他带我们去看了十世班禅的故居和孟达天池，看了一个山中温泉，还带我们去了一个远离常规路线的百年老村，那里有着精美木雕建筑。另外，还去了温都寺，在那里我们认识了他的一个喇嘛朋友。

这名司机热心周到，无可挑剔。他完成了给我们当导游的任务后，出乎意料地又来到我们所住的旅馆，开车把我们送到下一个目的地，没收我们一分钱。

2005 年，由于个人生活事情我陷入深深痛苦之时，一个朋友从上海打来电话说:“如果我明天去北京,你会在吗？”我想他只不过在安慰我，没想到第二天他真的出现在我面前。

“我觉得，需要有人跟你说说话，所以我就来了！”事实上，我确实需要找人倾诉倾诉。

2007 年，我退休离开岗位。虽然我可以以外国人的身份留在中国，但是我没有任何诸如养老金和医疗保险这样的福利。

我以前的一个学生住在杭州。他给我写信说：“我和我爱人都同意你来跟我们住，随便你住多久。你每天可以去西湖读书、写作。不需要你做什么，也不需要你付钱。”我当然不会顺水推舟接受这样的慷慨，但他们这种“对亲人般”的爱心和尊重，我将永远铭记在心。

在中国生活的岁月里，我也曾数次遭遇偷窃，也曾在自己不知情的情况下被人利用，被当作了腐败的工具。有人曾要求我，对我所知道的事情撒谎隐瞒。但是，我更愿铭记那些值得尊重的人。

In the name of the animals

I have always loved animals: they share a large part of our human nature. They don't attend school but have natural instincts and skills that several of us could envy.

Look at the bees… They have a perfectly structured society: queen, servants, nannies, workers. I would never intentionally crush an ant under my feet; who knows if it's not a messenger running to announce the starving colony a discovery of food! Buddhists pray every morning for the living creatures they might inadvertently kill during the day.

Birds of all kinds rejoice our eyes; they sing in the trees, and after years of observation, I have been raising 16 birds of four kinds in a large veranda which was their cage. I could understand their language. When, after my retirement, I started to travel for long periods, I had to give my birds to persons who – I made sure – would take care of them, not free them in the nature.

Birds and even butterflies know when it's time to migrate for winter, and they find their way back. An adult cat was given to a family living 10 km away. It was brought by car, at night. But two days later, it came back by itself to pick up its favorite blanket.

A dozen sparrows knock on my kitchen window every morning for their daily ration of rice.

Hearing that animal live shows would be banned soon across the country, I felt altogether astonished, deeply shocked and terribly angry.

以动物的名义

我一直很喜欢动物。人性的一大部分，动物也有。动物不需要上学，却有着让我们嫉妒的自然本能和技巧。

就说蜜蜂吧，它们的社会结构非常完美：有王后、仆从、奶妈、工人。我不会故意踩死蚂蚁，谁知道那是不是一只正在奔向饥饿的蚁群报告食物消息的信使呢？佛教徒每天早晨都要为他们白天不小心杀死的生灵祈祷。

各种各样的鸟愉悦我们的眼睛，它们在树丛中歌唱。我对鸟类观察好多年了，在一个很大的阳台间养了 4 种鸟，共 16 只。我能懂得它们的语言。退休以后，我开始长时间旅行，只好把鸟都送给了那些我知道会好好照顾它们的人，而没有把它们放归自然。

鸟，甚至蝴蝶，都知道什么时候迁徙他方过冬。它们也能找到回来的路。有一只猫被送给了10公里以外的人家，而且是在夜间用车送去的。但是两天以后，它自己又回到原来的家，去找它喜欢的小毯子。

在我厨房的窗口，每天早上都有一些麻雀敲打我的窗户讨要每日的米粒。

听说中国各地要禁止动物表演，我感到震惊，也很愤怒。

I strongly support the idea that circus animals as well as zoo animals must be treated well, with convenient and sufficient food, healthy and clean living spaces, and all the love and respect they deserve. However, in several situations, China tends to apply corrections instead of preventing faults, to punish instead of educating.

Zoos' original purpose is teaching people about the wonders of nature. Some tough animal welfare activists would like to deprive the society of the pleasure to admire wild animals in zoos. Once, a giraffe was fed plastic bags in a zoo, and died. In Beijing, a sadist poured petroleum in a bear's mouth on a scorching day. A tiger ripped off a little boy's arm, but the kid has passed the protective fence. Animal activists protested highly after each accident and asked for all the zoos to be closed.

Unlike zoo animals which are expensive to keep, show animals earn their living and also feed their owners' families. What will happen to the trainers and their families who, for generations in many cases, have known nothing else but working with animals? Where will they find work to survive? Who will pay for their children's education? They can't suddenly return to the employment market. Banning their means of earning a living is effectively banning them – honest citizens who deserve a decent life.

Astonishing show animals who (I consciously use "who" instead of "that") perform exciting and amazing actions before the public's wide open eyes are also wonders of nature, aren't they?

The ban aims at ending animal maltreatment. But the only example of possible danger mentioned in the one-page article published in *China Daily* (Nov. 23, 2010) is "tigers jumping through flaming rings, or bears playing with fire sticks". Should we ban cars from the roads because accidents occur? Should we stop people using

马戏团的动物和动物园的动物应该得到善待，对此我很支持。它们应该随时得到充足的食物，住在干净的地方，得到人的爱护和尊敬。可是，在极端的情况下，中国似乎更注重矫正，惩治多于教诲，而不是防患于未然。

设立动物园本来的目的是为了让人们了解大自然的奇妙。一些态度强硬的动物权利活动分子却要剥夺大家在动物园欣赏野生动物的乐趣。一次，一只长颈鹿因为吃了塑料袋而死亡。在北京，一个虐待狂在大热天把汽油倒进熊的嘴里。一只老虎曾经咬掉了一个男孩的胳膊，但是原因是那个男孩越过了栏杆。每次这样的事件发生后，动物保护主义者便发出抗议，呼吁关闭动物园。

动物园饲养动物的费用确实不菲，而马戏团则不然。马戏团的动物靠劳动养活自己，而且养活主人一家。有的驯兽师几代人只和动物打交道。取缔马戏团，对他们来说将意味着什么？他们将在哪里谋生？他们孩子的学费从何而来？他们不可能马上返回就业市场。取缔他们的营生，就等于取缔了老老实实的公民过像样生活的权利。

马戏团动物的精彩表演让观众眼界大开，这难道不也是大自然的奇迹吗？

这个禁令意在禁止虐待动物现象的发生，《中国日报》上一篇文章（2010 年 11 月 23 日）提到的危险表演仅限于“老虎钻火圈”和“狗熊耍火棒”。汽车也出事故，难道我们要禁止汽车吗？家用电器会引起火

electrical appliances because they may cause a fire? Would it be a good idea to lay off all firemen because of the danger inherent in their work? An accident occurred during the recent Asiad; a horse fell, broke its neck and died. Shouldn't we ban equestrian events from sports competitions?

Some animals may have been beaten during their training; these things obviously happen. But some kids are abused by their parents and teachers. Why not to ban school then? Or better: attack the root of the problem and forbid families to give birth?

Activists want to end animal maltreatment. Who could disagree? But the show animals – monkeys, lions, bears, dogs, ducks, etc. – actually thousands across the country can't be "recycled". Wild animals, once tamed, can't be sent back to the forest. Domestic animals such as dogs could be kept in families, but their owners will soon be unemployed and their animals will no longer have the right to work. Where will they find the money to survive? Zoos have their quota and can't buy up surplus animals. If the ban is implemented, animals will end up abandoned. Or will be killed.

The ban is one of the most ridiculous things I have heard of in China. Instead of a total ban, squads of inspectors should be dispatched to find those keepers and trainers who don't respect their animals, and fine or even imprison them. This would give work opportunity to some of the unemployed rather than increasing their number.

Performing animals like their trainers and like the public. They are receptive to applauses and cries of admiration. They know when they have done well, and they are proud to go and get their reward of a fish or a cookie.

I sincerely hope that the government will revise its position before it is too late. If the ban can't be retracted completely, it should be

灾，难道我们要禁止使用吗？消防员的工作很危险，难道我们要把他们都解雇吗？亚运会上，一匹马跌倒后摔断脖子死了，难道我们就因此取消赛马吗？

有些动物在训练中可能挨过打，这种事情显然发生过。但是家长和老师也打过孩子。为什么不把学校也关闭了？或者干脆釜底抽薪——禁止生孩子好了。

动物保护主义者要消灭虐待动物现象，大家都不会反对。但是马戏团的动物，诸如成千上万的猴子、狮子、狗熊、狗和鸭子等，不可能被“再循环使用”。野生动物一旦被驯化，就不可能放归山林。像狗这样的驯养动物，可以留在主人家里，但是主人不久即将失业，他们的动物也失去了表演的权利。这些人家赖以为生的收入将从何而来？动物园容纳动物数量是有限的，不能收购过多的动物。如果此项禁令得以实施，那些动物要么将被遗弃要么被杀掉。

这项禁令是我在中国听到的最为荒唐的事情之一。与其禁止动物表演，不如派人调查虐待动物的人和驯兽师，并处以罚款乃至监禁。这将给一些无业者提供工作机会，而不是增加失业人口。

表演类动物喜欢它们的主人和观众，也喜欢掌声和欢呼声。它们知道自己表演得很好，乐于骄傲地领取一条鱼或者一块饼干作为回报。

我真诚地希望政府能及时改变其立场。如果这个禁令不能取消，至少应该加以修改，那些聪明可爱的动物们也许就有生存机会了，而公众

modified at least. Maybe the lovely, clever and talented animals will be given a chance to survive, and the public will still have a chance to admire them. I would not like to see our century tainted with such a black spot in history.

"The greatness of a society and its moral progress can be judged by the way it treats its animals," Mahatma Gandhi once said.

也有机会去欣赏它们。我不希望我们这个世纪被玷污。

圣雄甘地就曾经说："一个社会是否伟大，道德是否进步，只要看其如何对待动物就可以知道了。"

Public transportation as a textbook

One of my three secrets for *Living Happily in China* (title of my newly published book) is taking the bus. What I've learned through public transportation in 20 years is incredible. Combining the Chinese wisdom to my Western "daring," I've become a sly passenger.

Last week, I took a bus that was shorter than the queue. The conductor – a young woman who cared for her passengers – was giving advices: "Please, don't push. Give a hand to the man with the baby." She was standing in front of the first seat which she kept for a *laotou* (elderly) or a pregnant woman.

I sneaked behind her and occupied the seat in all honesty. Then came a man, who might be in his late 50s. The conductor turned around telling the *laotou* to sit "here", and she saw me. Two question marks surged into her eyes. My ancestors in Italy must have gifted me with younger looks than my age... I clarified the situation, saying: "I'm also an elderly."

In such a crowded country, taking a bus requires technique and tricks. It's a daily adventure, unlike in Canada or the United States.

I live at Yinghuayuan, a community near the Capital Airport. Bus route 935, which runs to downtown Dongzhimen subway station, is the only bus that caters to the thousands of Yinghuayuan households.

Recently, to shorten the commuting time for those who go directly to the downtown area, an express route was added, which has fewer stops than the original route. People wait in two parallel queues. For some, it makes no difference to take one or the other bus. When a fast bus becomes visible, some people waiting in the ordinary bus line would switch to the fast bus line, and vice versa. This is not a big offence, as they have been queuing anyway.

我的公交大课堂

在自己新近出版的《在中国幸福生活》一书中，我谈到三个秘密，其中之一是乘坐公交。二十多年来，我乘公交所学到的东西令人难以置信。我把中国人的智慧和西方人的“胆量”结合到一起，使自己成为了一个乘车老手。

上星期，我乘坐了一辆巴士。乘客排的队比车还长。售票员是一个女青年，很关心自己的乘客。她劝告乘客们：“别挤别挤，请为抱孩子的让个座。”她站在第一排座位前面，要把它留给一个老人或者孕妇。

我绕过她，心安理得地坐下来。后来，上来一个男的，将近六十岁的样子。售票员转过身来，对老头说您坐在“这里”，可是她发现我已经坐在那儿了。她的两个眼睛变成了两个问号。

肯定是因为我的意大利祖先的基因让我的容貌显得年轻，我不得不澄清一下说：“我也是老人。”

在中国这个不少地方都拥挤不堪的国家，乘公交车得需要点技巧和诡计。每天乘车都如同探险，这跟在加拿大或者美国不同。

我住在樱花园，首都机场附近的小区。这个小区几千户人家都依靠开往东直门地铁站的 935 路公交车。

最近，为了缩短人们去市区的时间，增加了一趟快车，只停几个站。乘客排两队等车。对有的人来说，乘坐慢车和快车没什么区别，所以快车来的时候，有些排在慢车队的人就换到快车队来。反过来也是一样。这样做并不冒犯他人，因为大家都排队了。

To secure a precious seat, some passengers would take the trouble of walking to the precedent stop to take the bus, which is not at all an offence.

What I find really hard to get used to is that there are always so many people who never queue up.

My neighbors have become civilized recently: They have learned the word *paidui* (queue). Well… except 70 percent of them. Some people probably carry iron in their bags, as the approaching bus seems to draw them like a magnet. They may be in the queue or they may have just arrived, but the sight of a bus would immediately propels them to move forward, little by little or all at once, to be closer to the door.

The others who still follow the queue would grumble, or criticize those doing wrong. Amazingly, half of the offenders would go back to their place.

Yesterday, two women in their 40s arrived as the bus drew nearer and they ran in front of the 30-or-so people queuing in order. Several discontent people reproached them. But, in China, people usually don't want to openly offend a total stranger. The tough nuts continued to chat and joke between them, turning a deaf ear to the protests. The two women were the first to get on the bus, though people continued to mutter that "their *suzhi* (moral quality) was very low". Neither did the conductor, who witnessed their wrongdoing, intervene.

I was among the three of four people who didn't have a seat. I felt cheated. Although it's not polite in our culture to make observations on someone's behavior, I gathered all my courage and went directly to the two women. In a trembling but sweet voice I said: "You have not queued up, have you? So, please let me sit, and this old man, too." The whole bus looked at this drama. The two said nothing and got up.

If you think they blushed, you're too generous. As the Chinese saying goes, their face was thicker than the corner of the city wall.

为了得到一个座位，有的乘客往回走一站乘车，这同样也并不冒犯别人。

我习惯不了的是，总是有很多人根本不排队。

我的邻居最近变文明了：他们学会了排队这个词。但排队的只有30%。有些人的包里似乎背有铁块，因为公共汽车一到来，他们就像被磁铁吸引着涌过去。他们也许在排队，也许刚刚赶到，但一看到公交车，他们就开始向前蠕动，一点一点的跟大家一起向车门靠近。

其他还在排队的人就会抱怨，或者批评那些做错事的人。奇妙的是，一半的人会回到原来的位子。

昨天，正当汽车进站的时候，有两名四十来岁的妇女来到车站。她们跑起来，跑到排队等车的三十多人前头。有些人表示不满，开始斥责她们。可中国人一般不会去冒犯一个陌生人，那两个厚脸皮的人自顾自说说笑笑，对人们的批评充耳不闻。她们抢在前头上了车。后边的人嘟嘟囔囔地指责她们"素质太低。"售票员目睹了一切，却没有干预。

最后有三四个人没有占到座位，我是其中之一。我觉得很冤。虽然在我自己的文化中，对别人的行为品头论足是不礼貌的，但我还是鼓起勇气，直接走到那两个女人前面，用颤抖但是和气的声音说："你们没有排队，对吧？那么请让我坐下，还有这位老人。"全车的人都等着看这场戏怎么收场，那两个女人无言以对，站了起来。

如果你以为她们会脸红，那你就太宽厚了，就像中国俗语说的，她们的脸比城墙还厚。

Dog regulation necessary

Shanghai, a city of 6,400 sq. km and 20 million people, has about 1 million dogs. AFP reported that in 2009 about 164,000 dog owners had got licenses for about 200,000 dogs, that is, only 20 percent of what many say is the actual number.

Shanghai recorded on average 100,000 dog attacks a year since 2006, up to 140,000 in 2009. This is where Shanghai is different from Paris or New Zealand.

According to the World Health Organization, more than 55,000 people die of rabies across the world every year, and China is second only to India on the list of countries with the highest number of rabies deaths.

Though rabies can be prevented if people have their dogs vaccinated, a 2009 BioMed Central report said that 60 percent of the Chinese cities it surveyed had a vaccination rate of less than 70 percent. The (Shanghai) draft suggested that fine for unregistered dogs would be of 1,000 yuan. It is still not enough to convince all owners to accept the law.

Deng Zixin, a deputy to the Shanghai city people's congress, told the Xinhua News Agency that the dog ownership problem "was getting out of hand". If dog ownership is not better managed, dogs could become a bigger nuisance for people with their barking, biting and littering. Perhaps this is why Shanghai is set to follow Chengdu and Guangzhou in allowing one household to own only one dog from next year.

In the compound where I live, 60 percent of the households have at least one dog. In my building, two out of the eight occupied apartments have respectively four and five dogs, the others, one dog, and only mine has none.

养狗需要立规矩

上海面积有 6400 平方公里，人口 2000 万，大约有 100 万只狗。法新社报道，2009 年大约有 16.4 万养犬人为 20 万只狗领了准养证。很多人认为，这仅仅是狗实际数量的五分之一。

2006 年以来，上海狗伤人事故平均每年 10 万起，2009 年达到 14 万起。这也是上海与巴黎和新西兰之间一个很大的不同。

世界卫生组织统计，每年世界上有 5.5 万人死于狂犬病，印度最多，中国次之。

虽然可以通过给狗注射疫苗预防狂犬病。根据生物医学中心 2009 年的一项报告，该中心在中国进行调查后发现，60% 的城市的犬类免疫率低于 70%。上海市一项立法草案建议，每只未注册的狗罚款 1000 元，但这还不足以有效约束所有养犬人。

上海市人大代表邓子新对新华社记者说，养狗问题已经“难以收拾”。如果对养狗缺乏更好的管理，狗的吠叫、撕咬、随地便溺都会给人们带来很大困扰。因此，继成都和广州之后，上海将出台一户只许养一只犬的规定。

我所住的小区内，60% 的人家每家至少有一条狗。在我住的楼里，8 户人家中有一家养了 4 只，另一家养了 5 只，其余各家也都有一只，唯独我没养。

Raising a dog became popular in the late 1990s as the life standard improved radically. If, as the draft regulation on keeping dogs recommends, the authorities allow one household to keep only one dog, many people are likely to continue having several dogs but registering just one of them. They will exercise them in secret – or not at all. How that will work is a real problem.

In a move to encourage people to register their pets, the fees came down from 2,000 yuan in Shanghai city center and 1,000 in the suburbs to only 300 yuan, vaccination and ID card included. Fine for unregistered dogs, instead, would be of 1,000 yuan, still not enough to convince all owners to accept the law.

The draft law suggests that the number of dogs a family can own may depend on the size of its house, and its proximity to open spaces. Similarly, Shanghai and other large Chinese cities have begun to question their one-child policy, could they allow wealthy families to have more than one offspring?

The new law aroused initial opposition from the public after rumors that unclaimed stray dogs were to be put down after 30 days. The situation was clarified by an official, who explained that only dogs infected with diseases like rabies would be put to sleep and that the draft was blank on how the rest of the caught dog would be treated.

As I see it, the regulation is not the prelude to a mass cull of dogs. There are legal and humane ways to keep the number of dogs under control. Sterilization is easy, and one of the safest methods. Sure, it comes at a cost, but the expense is just one of many associated with keeping a dog. It is important that pet owners understand its advantages.

Stray dogs and cats wander the streets because irresponsible people abandon them. Pet ownership comes with a moral responsibility towards living beings.

All laws curtail the freedom of some for the greater benefit of society. I see nothing inhumane in the draft.

The new regulations, if properly enforced, should avoid future problems. But there still remains the issue of what do to about the existing surplus of dogs.

上个世纪90年代末，人们养狗成风。那时，中国人的生活水平大幅度提高。如果按照上海地方法规草案“一户一犬”的规定，可能会出现本来养了好几条狗，却只登记一条的现象。他们会秘密遛狗，或者干脆不遛了。这项草拟中的法规将如何实施还真是一个问题。

为了鼓励养犬人进行宠物登记，上海市区的登记费从2000元降到1000元，郊区则只有300元，其中包括了免疫和身份卡的费用。对不登记者罚款1000元，显然不足以使所有养犬人遵守这项法规。

对这项草案有人建议，每户养犬数量可根据住房面积、与公共场所的距离而有所区别。

有传言说，新的法规将规定，流浪狗30天无人认领将被处死。这引起了公众的反对。一个官员出来澄清说，只对有病的狗，比如有狂犬病的狗，才这样处理。其他流浪狗怎么处理，草案没有提及。

据我看，这个法案并不会导致对狗进行大规模清理。要控制狗的数量，可以找到既合法，也合乎人道的办法：宠物实施绝育既方便又安全。当然，这种手术要花钱，但这是养狗的必要花费之一。让养犬人明白这样做的好处很重要。

流浪狗和流浪猫在街上乱跑乱窜，是因为不负责任的主人抛弃了它们。养宠物的主人对生命负有道德责任。

所有的法律都是为了全社会的更大利益而对部分自由进行限制。我认为，这个法案没有什么不人道的地方。

这项新的法规如果执行适当，就可以避免出现问题。不过，到底怎么处理多余的狗，还真是一个问题。

Lunar New Year gains in status

I always like to send my wishes to friends on their birthdays, as our birthday is the only day out of 365 that belongs to us in a very special way. My Western friends used to thank me, adding "Could you check what my Chinese sign is?" or "I was told I'm a Horse, what are the features of that zodiac sign in China?"

Through the 20 years I have spent in China, I have seen a growing interest among Western people for the Chinese 12-year cycle, each year attributed to an animal, for *Chunjie* which is the Chinese lunar New Year, and for all kinds of symbols and activities related to the Chinese zodiac system. Among those details are the red fabric belt that one wears during *benmingnian* (or the year of "your animal"), the story of why these animals were chosen and why in "this order", the reason why the Chinese pay so much importance to the year of a person's birth and the way to ask a person's age in Chinese, and the long noodles that should one not miss on a birthday for a long life.

There are paper cuts, too, featuring the 12 animals, so light and easy to include into a letter that I have sent more than 200 around the world during my time in China.

The Chinese lunar New Year is now celebrated in many countries that have a strong Chinese community. Foreign TV show anchors do not miss the opportunity to offer their best wishes.

Several countries, including Canada, have started producing special postage stamps for the Chinese *Chunjie*. Some of my friends send them to me and ask questions about the pattern or about some elements they don't understand. Sometimes, I just have to refer them to one of my books, as I have written a lot about Chinese culture. It seems that the world is becoming increasingly interested in Chinese culture.

春节地位节节高

我总喜欢在朋友的生日给他们送去我的祝愿，因为生日是一年当中对我们具有特殊意义的一天。我的西方朋友们在对我表示感谢的同时总是要问："我的中国生肖是什么？"或者，"有人说我属马，这个属相有什么特点？"

在中国二十多年，我感到西方人对中国的十二生肖，对中国的春节，对与属相相关的各种吉祥物和活动的兴趣越来越浓厚。提出的问题有：十二生肖动物及其排序有何来历，中国人为什么在本命年要系红腰带，为什么对出生的年份那么看重，为什么生日的长寿面不可或缺，怎么用中文问年龄，等等。

中国有十二生肖的剪纸，非常精美，夹在信里寄给朋友很方便。在中国二十多年，我给朋友寄过的剪纸有 200 多张。

在国外，凡有华人聚集的地方，中国的春节都很热闹。外国电视台的主持人也会不失时机地向观众祝贺新春。

在有些国家，包括加拿大，还为中国春节发行纪念邮票。有些朋友把这种邮票寄给我，问我那些图案的意思和有关的问题。有的时候，我告诉他们参考我写的书，因为我写的许多文章都与中国文化有关。看来，世界对中国文化越来越感兴趣了。

Japan, South Korea, Mongolia, Vietnam and other Asian countries have a 12-animal calendar which may differ a little from the Chinese calendar. For instance, the rabbit may be replaced with the cat.The Dai, one of the ethnic groups in China, include the elephant in their calendar. But Western people generally call them all "Chinese calendar".

Bronze heads of the twelve animals which decorated the clepsydra fountain of a western palace in Beijing's Yuanmingyuan were taken by English and French invaders during the Second Opium War in 1860. Still, they are considered treasures of the country and China is trying to get them back one by one.

The Chinese zodiac has long been used to predict a person's future and character. Sometimes, I am asked whether Chinese people really believe in the influence of a specific animal on their child's life. In all cultures and religions, symbols and practices exist that people follow without necessarily believing in them. For instance, persons born in the year of the Rabbit are said to be "virtuous, conscientious and well organized". The rabbit has a symbolic value in the West as well. Because of its fertility, it symbolizes prosperity.

Even in today's China, matrimonial arrangements are often based on the compatibility between the signs of a couple. Parents may ask an astrologer to examine the "sky map" (or horoscope) of the would-be brides and grooms in a way to bring happiness into their married life. Specific knowledge is required to interpret the "sky map" and calculate the celestial or heavenly stems, the earthly branches, the yin and yang, and the five elements (fire, earth, metal, water and wood).

People assume that children born in the year of the Monkey will be clever, supple and passionate. On contrary, the year of the Goat is "not" good for girls especially. So, fewer births were recorded in the year of the Goat, and the following year (of the Monkey) saw a baby boom.

But after social changes and improvement in education levels, more people see the zodiac signs as fun rather than determining factors of a person's fate.

日本、韩国、蒙古、越南和亚洲其他国家和地区也有十二生肖，但与中国的略有不同。例如，属兔的可能变成属猫的，中国少数民族之一傣族的傣历生肖里则有大象。

在 1860 年第二次鸦片战争中，英法联军盗走了北京圆明园里大水法十二兽首铜像。这些兽首乃是中国的国宝，中国正在想办法一个个地收回来。

在中国,人们很早就利用星相来预测人的性格和命运。有人曾问我，中国人是否真相信属相对自己孩子生活会有影响。各种文化和宗教里，都有一些象征符号和习俗。 人们尊崇这些习俗，并不表明一定真诚相信。例如，中国人说属兔的人“有德行，组织力强”。在西方，兔子则象征多子多孙。

直到如今，中国人在婚姻上常常考虑男女双方的属相。父母会请算命先生测算新娘、新郎的属相是否相配，以求婚后生活幸福。算命需要有关于天干地支、阴阳五行等方面的特别知识。

人们认为，猴年生的孩子聪明、灵活、富有感情，而羊年出生的则相反，特别是女孩子命运不佳。所以，羊年出生的孩子数量就很少，而接下来的猴年则会有很多孩子出生。

但是随着社会的发展进步，人们教育水平的提高，越来越多的人只是把属相当作好玩的事情，而不再看作是决定人生的因素了。

Fengshui is another Chinese cultural phenomenon. It is not recognized officially but many people – even in the West – tend to believe in it. Globalization has not been a one-way traffic. If more people in the West today believe in the Chinese zodiac and *fengshui*, an increasingly number of Chinese today celebrate Christmas and Halloween, and Chinese women wear white wedding gowns.

Such cultural interaction results from the high status China enjoys in today's world thanks to its fast and energetic economic development. Globalization is unavoidable; therefore, it's natural for cultural exchanges to be more intensive.

It is reported that 40 million non-Chinese people are learning the Chinese language across the world as of January 2010. And I think the number of people interested in China and its culture will increase steadily.

“风水”也是中国文化的一部分。风水没有获得正经学问的地位，但是有很多人，甚至西方人也都相信。全球化并非单行道。如今，越来越多的西方人相信中国的属相和风水，越来越多的中国人则过起圣诞节和万圣节，女人结婚也穿起白色婚纱。

中国经济快速蓬勃发展，中国的国际地位不断增高，因此中西文化交流进一步增强。全球化难以避免，文化交流也将会日益密切。

据报道,截至2010年1月,全世界学习汉语的非中国人达到4000万。我认为，对中国和中国文化感兴趣的人会越来越多。

A city without peddlers

I love peddlers. I mean I love what peddlers sell. No, what I really mean is that I love the atmosphere of a city with peddlers.

When my mother visited Beijing in 1995, the Fourth World Conference on Women was about to start in the Chinese capital, and all the illegal peddlers had been banned from downtown. Some had been returned to their native rural place where their *hukou* (residence registration) was, and others ousted back to their makeshift household in the city's outskirt, deprived of their earning until the end of the international event and summoned to remain invisible. The same process occurs before each major activity in modern cities, such as the 2008 Olympics ban which produced a more durable effect.

There was a time I used to buy corn on the cob at Dongzhimen long distance bus terminal when I returned home. At late evening, vendors packed six or eight remaining cobs in a plastic bag which they sold only one yuan. The cobs were small and bad looking, but the most tasteful. I didn't eat them on the bus. They kept my hands warm, and once at home, I reheated the corn and brushed butter and salt on it. What a treat!

I also liked to buy fresh flowers: twenty mini-roses for eight yuan, after bargaining, was a good deal. At that price, I could offer myself such pleasure in continuation.

On summer evenings, I liked to take a walk at sunset when the perfume of pineapples filled the air. Not only vendors offered the juicy and sweet fruits but also the peeling service.

Other vendors sold DVDs. I never stop at their stalls, as buying pirated films means stealing the artists' legitimate earnings. Now that I have no other income but what I earn from my free-lance pen, I know

没有小贩的城市

我喜欢小贩，我是说我喜欢小贩卖的东西。不，我真正的意思是我喜欢有小贩的城市气息。

1995年，我母亲来中国的时候，正赶上第四届世界妇女大会在北京召开。所有的无照摊贩，都禁止上街摆摊。有的被遣返到户口所在的农村，有的则须回到郊区他们自己搭建的房子。在这次国际活动结束之前，他们将无钱可赚。他们变成了隐形人。这种现象在各大城市举行重要活动之前都会发生，比如2008年奥运会，禁止小贩上街的规定执行的时间更长。

有一段时间，在回家的路上，我常常在东直门长途汽车站买玉米棒子。傍晚时分，小贩们常常把没有卖出去的玉米放到一个塑料袋里，每个袋子里装六到八个，只卖一元钱。这种玉米比较小，样子也不太好看，但是味道特别好。在车上，我没有吃，只用它们焐手。到家以后，我把玉米加热，抹上黄油和盐，味道好极了。

我还喜欢买鲜花，讲价以后可以8元钱买12枝小玫瑰，很合算的。这种价格可以让我长期享受这一乐趣。

夏天的傍晚，我喜欢在日落时分出去散步，去感受空气中弥漫的菠萝香味。小贩们出售的菠萝汁多味甜，他们还负责给你削皮。

也有小贩在卖DVD。我从来不去他们的摊位，因为买盗版电影光

what intellectual property rights means, and I don't do to others what I would not like them to do to me.

But flowers and corn are not faked! They have not been grown illegally on IPR protected land. They don't contain dangerous substances. Pineapples have ripened on the plant and have traveled from the south by train, and from the train station to Beijing streets on manpower-activated carts. Why have the vendors been chased, while the DVD sellers have their place under a roof in subway stations and other establishments?

Along the main street of my living area in Shunyi, every afternoon after 3 pm, peasants install their cart and start selling apples, frozen fish, leeks, carrots, roasted chestnuts, small engraved gourds, dry raisin, etc. Sometimes, I do buy; but when I hear the police warning from their loudspeaker that vendors are given two minutes to disappear, otherwise they will be arrested, I suddenly remember that, in fact, they have no permit to sell along the street, and that we have a huge covered market at 200 steps away, where the prices are higher because the legal vendors pay a rent. But our policemen are quite soft-hearted with peddlers. Or maybe they feel too cold to get off their cars.

Those who sell counterfeit *fapiao* have no material to move when police is around, and they run fast.

However, it seems to me that Tibetans – from Qinghai, Lhasa or Gansu – are given more chances. In their colorful attires, wearing ringing jewelry and brilliantly ornate hats, they are certainly visible. Though some of them sell endangered animals' skin or horns, most of the time they display exclusively inoffensive merchandises such as Tibetan-silver earrings and bracelets. Police seems to ignore their presence at Madianqiao underground passage, outside the Sanyuanqiao subway station, and inside the Dongzhimen station.

I'm not claiming an enforcement of the ban on peddlers; on contrary, I would like the same "chance" to be given to those who don't infringe any property rights when selling flowers, corn and pineapples.

碟就相当于窃取艺术家合法的收入。现在我没有别的收入，只是靠自由写作为生，我知道版权意味着什么。己所不欲，不施于人。

可鲜花和玉米就不同了，它们不是非法地种植在受版权保护的土地上，也不含有害成分。菠萝是成熟后从南方用火车运来的，到了北京车站后，小贩再用人力车拉到街上去卖。为什么卖菠萝的小贩被赶走了，而卖 DVD 的在地铁站或别的地方却有一席之地呢？

在顺义我住所附近的主要街道上，每天下午三点后，农民们用车拉着苹果、冻鱼、黄鳝、胡萝卜、炒栗子、葫芦工艺品和葡萄干等出售。我有时也在那里买东西。可当我听到警察用扩音喇叭警告他们两分钟之内必须收摊，否则就要抓人时，我突然意识到他们都是无照摊贩。200步以外就有一个菜市场，但那里的价格比较高，因为有照摊贩要交租金。不过警察对小贩倒不算严厉，或许是因为他们不愿意在大冷天从车里出来吧。

卖假发票的人没有什么要搬运。警察来了，他们溜得最快。

可是据我观察，来自青海、拉萨和甘肃的藏族人做生意的机会更多。他们穿着鲜艳的服装，戴着叮当响的首饰和装饰漂亮的帽子，在大街上非常显眼。虽然他们中有人在卖濒危动物的皮毛和犄角，但大部分人卖的还是合法商品，比如藏银耳环和手镯。他们在马甸桥地下通道、三元桥和东直门地铁站摆摊。警察对他们似乎视而不见。

我并不主张禁止小贩，相反支持给那些卖鲜花、玉米和菠萝这类合法商品的小贩同样做生意的机会。

Questioning retirement age

In Canada, retirement age for both genders is 65. Persons who, on their own choice, retire earlier must generally wait to the age of 65 for getting their pension.

When I arrived in China, I made a double amazing discovery: The age was different for men and women, and Chinese retired as early as 60 and 55 respectively. I thought – at that time – that is was nice to retire when one is still young and has strength for travelling, learning painting, read all the books one had no time to read before, and meet with friends.

I also thought that women were advantaged by the system as they could enjoy free life five years younger than their male counterparts. This could be right 25 years ago, but today, people have an easier life and eat better; they are still vigorous at 60. What if they are forced to retire?

Lifespan has increased significantly in the last three decades. Would retirement pension be enough to cover people's longer life?

Nowadays, I see women's retirement at 55 as a segregationist measure: women are pushed out of the work market though they are still capable, and at an age when they could fully use their work experience and skills. This measure deprives society of talents on the one hand, and, on the other hand, deprives women from getting a higher pension would they retire later. Although some officially retired women continue to work three, four years, for their former employer, but during this period, they are not allowed to contribute to their pension plan. When they effectively retire, their allowance is calculated on the years they worked before retirement.

也谈退休年龄

在加拿大，男女法定退休年龄都是 65 岁。如果愿意提前退休，必须等到 65 岁才能领取养老金。

我刚到中国的时候，有件事让我倍感吃惊:不但男女退休年龄不同，而且退休年龄也早于加拿大:男的60,女的55。当时我想,趁着年轻退休，那就有精力去旅游、学习、作画，读以前没有时间看的书，与朋友聚会，等等，那该多好啊!

当时我认为，中国的退休制度安排对女士给予更多关照，与男士比起来，她们可以提前 5 年享受退休生活。25 年前，这可能是真的。但如今生活变好了，人们 60 岁的时候仍然精力充沛。如果 60 岁就让他们退休，会怎么样呢?

三十年来，人们的寿命显著增长。寿命延长了，有足够的退休金支付多出来的费用吗?

我现在认为，安排妇女在 55 岁退休，有性别歧视成分：在妇女还能工作，还能利用她们的工作经验和技能的时候，把她们强行推出就业市场。 这种政策一方面不利于社会使用人才，另一方面剥夺了妇女获得更高退休金的机会。虽然有些正式退休的妇女被原单位返聘，但返聘期间的工作对其退休金的基数不起作用。她们不再工作时，其退休金仍然按照她们正式退休时的工龄来计算。

Something is wrong in the system as some professionals such as hematologists or cardiologists are obliged by their employer to continue to work even past 70 years of age, though they are tired and ill, because of a dearth of staff in the profession.

Retirement age could remain low (60) as the work market must absorb the young generation – a huge number.

Allowing early retirement is one thing, but forcing people to retire is quite another. I think major changes should be implemented. First: retirement age should be the same for men and women. Second: people should be free to continue three-five more years if they wish, with allowed contribution to their pension plan. Third: no one should be forced to work after the limit age if it is not their will.

有些专业人士，比如说血液病专家或心脏病专家，因为本行业人才的缺乏，年过 70 岁单位还要求他们继续工作，而她们则已疲惫多病。这说明这种人事安排本身存在问题。

我认为，为了就业市场能够吸纳大量年轻的劳动力，则可以把退休年龄定得低一些（比如 60 岁）。

但是，许可人们提早退休是一回事，强迫退休是另外一回事。我认为，应该进行重大的改革：首先，退休年龄应该男女一样；其次，如果人们愿意多工作三五年，应该允许，并且他们的退休金应该按照实际退休的年龄计算；第三，如果到了退休年龄，职工不想继续工作，不应强迫他们推迟退休。

To be or not to be a Tiger Mother

In her book *Battle Hymn of the Tiger Mother*, Amy Chua, a law professor at Yale University, shares her parenting techniques and explains why she doesn't approve the self-esteem-style form of education which holds that "learning should be fun, that rote repetition destroys the soul, and that children should be encouraged to discover their own individuality and interests", calling all this "rubbish".

I think Chua is an extremist in her judgements, especially when she says: "Western parents romanticize the idea of pursuing passions and giving your kid choices. If you give a 10-year-old the choice to pursue his or her passion, for them it's going to be [getting on] Facebook for six hours," adding that she consciously chose to take the Eastern parenting path. But it is not a matter of East and West, and nuances should be made.

I was the first child of my parents, and was raised in an extremely strict way. There was a difference of nine years between me and the last child, and there was also a huge difference in our education style. Not only at home but at school, girls of my generation were forbidden to wear pants or shorts (only skirts), shoes with medium-high heels, to use lipstick and nail polish, or to talk with a male classmate if not in presence of others. I was not allowed to attend summer camps organized by the school except after my teachers convinced my parents, in secret, that the camp would be only girls and that two teachers would supervise the camp. Later, when I became a teacher, I also talked secretly with immigrant parents of my students for the same reason. In my family, no TV was permitted on school days, and we could only see two programs during the weekend. No sleepovers, no parties. Just like "Tiger Mom" Amy Chua's daughters.

子女教育说“虎妈”

耶鲁大学法学教授蔡美儿在其《虎妈战歌》中与读者分享了她的育子心得，声言她不赞成一味强调孩子自尊的教育方式。她认为，所谓“学习应该有乐趣，死记硬背摧残心灵，应当鼓励孩子发展个性和兴趣”等一些说法都是“垃圾”。

我认为蔡美儿的论断过于极端，特别是她说：“西方的父母让孩子由着性情自己选择，并且对这种做法抱着十分浪漫的想法。如果你让一个 10 岁的孩子任意选择，那就是每天 6 个小时泡在社交网络‘脸书’之上。”她特别强调她有意选择了东方教子方式。但是，育子问题不是东西方之分那么简单，细微的差别还是要加以区分。

我是家里的第一个孩子。父母对我的要求及其严格。我比家里最小的孩子大 9 岁。父母对我们的教育方式也有很大不同。我那一辈的女孩子，无论在家里，还是在社会上，都不允许穿裤子（只能穿裙子），不许穿中高跟鞋、抹口红、染指甲，不许单独跟男生说话。家里还不允许我参加夏令营，多亏老师私下跟父母说，夏令营里都是女孩子，而且有两名老师负责夏令营的监管工作，这才得以成行。我当了老师以后，曾经因为同样的情况我也私下跟移民孩子的家长沟通过。在家里，只有周末我们才能看电视，周末的时候也只能看两套节目。我们不可以在朋友家过夜，不许参加派对。我们的情况跟虎妈的女儿们一样。

My mother was extremely harsh because she was afraid we had turned bad. She lost her mother when she was only 12, married at 18, and had examples in the family of youths whose behavior was far from ideal. When, later, I told her how much I suffered, she maintained that she was right, as her method had brought good results.

Was I happy? No. The worst thing for me was to be living in an environment where other girls had less strict parents. Still, there is a difference between a free-for-all and an education allowing a child to make decisions based on morality, self-respect, and reasonable freedom. When Lulu and Sophia Chua are asked whether they are "happy", they answer in a philosophical way – avoiding blaming their mother.

An important skill in parenting is to explain to children why you want them to do something and why you forbid them to do other things. If you tell a child "Don't touch!" you only encourage him to touch.

Amy Chua forced her daughters to learn violin and piano and to practice three hours a day. My father decided that I would learn a musical instrument but let me choose which one, after listening to concerts with me and making suggestions. I chose piano, and studied it for eight years, up to four hours a day, not imposed but because I understood intensive practice was necessary to progress.

When my children were in primary school, I obliged them to choose one extra-curriculum activity in sport (baseball, football, swimming) and one in art (folk dance, drawing, music). A rule was set: you *finish* the session you start. If you like it, you can continue; if not, you can change. I would tolerate no abandonment. My son chose gardening once, and regretted it half-way. To encourage him to continue to the end, I offered to buy the vegetables he would bring home and paid him the market price.

因为担心我们学坏，我母亲对我们特别严厉。她 12 岁的时候，我外婆去世。她 18 岁就结婚了，对有些家庭中孩子行为不当的情况有所体会。后来我告诉她，在她的管教下我曾经多么痛苦。她坚持认为自己的做法正确，因为她教育出的孩子是成功的。

那时我感到幸福吗？不。我感觉最糟糕的是，周围女孩的父母都比较宽容。但是，完全放任孩子，与允许孩子在道德、自尊与合理自由的基础上做出决定，这两种教育方式之间还是有区别的。当有人问起蔡美儿的两个女儿蔡思慧和蔡思珊是否“幸福”时,她们很策略地作了回答，避免去指责自己的母亲。

育子的一个重要技巧是要让孩子明白他们为什么要做某件事，为什么不许做某件事。如果你只告诉孩子“别动那个”，这其实等于鼓励他们那样做。

蔡美儿强迫女儿学习小提琴和钢琴，每天练习 3 个小时。我的父亲也认为我应该学一种乐器，但是他带我去听音乐会，给我提出建议，最后让我自己选择学什么。我选择了钢琴，练习了 8 年，每天 4 个小时。我不是被迫的，我懂得只有加强练习才能取得进步。

我的孩子们上小学时，我让他们在课外体育运动（棒球、足球或者游泳）和课外文艺活动（民间舞蹈、绘画或音乐）中分别各选一种。我给他们立了一条规则:一旦要学,就要学完一期。如果喜欢,可以继续学。如果不喜欢,可以换一种。我不会容忍他们放弃。我的儿子选择了园艺，但中途后悔了。为了鼓励他学下去，我提出按照市场价格收购他带回家的蔬菜。

I don't agree with Amy Chua when she says that "children on their own never want to work, which is why it is crucial in the decision to override their preferences." If children do what they have chosen, if they like what they do and are guided by caring parents, they will sustain their efforts to succeed.

Amy Chua didn't allow her daughters to not be the No. 1 students in every subject (except gym and drama). It's true that Sophia Chua recently debuted at Carnegie Hall as a concert pianist. Tiger Mom's view on happiness is that if her daughters are successful, they will be happy; and that the strict education she gives the girls will provide them with the tools to be happy. However, this can be true only if she succeeded in transplanting the idea in her daughters' minds that "success equals happiness".

Chua's own parents thought an A- was not good enough, and she never questioned that. She explained that what Chinese parents should convey to their child is not "You must get A, otherwise I won't like you," but on contrary, "I believe in you so much, I know that you can be excellent." Believing in a child's capacity is a good point. But if all children theoretically can do their best, not all can be top-ranked performers.

I have been a high school teacher for 28 years in Canada. Following an event which demonstrated the importance for a student to feel he/she is loved, I revaluated my relationship with each of my 120 students, and found at least one chance to tell each one, or to write positive words on their assignments such as "I like you because…", "I truly appreciate when you…". But I never ask low performers to do more than they are capable of. Instead, I take the philosophy that "If you really can't do better, it is ok; if you can, I believe you will!" Not everyone needs to be the first in the class or have the highest marks. The most important thing is to "be the best you can be."

我也不赞同蔡美儿的说法：“如果由着孩子的性子，他们永远不想去工作，所以在做决定的时候不能听任他们自己随意选择。”我认为，如果孩子们喜欢做自己选择的事情，再加上细心父母的指导，他们就会努力坚持下去。

蔡美儿要求孩子，除了体育和戏剧，所有课程都要拿第一。蔡思慧果真在卡内基音乐厅进行了钢琴独奏演出。虎妈的幸福观就是，女儿如果成功，那就幸福。她对女儿进行严格教育，就是为了她们得到幸福。但是，虎妈只有让女儿真正接受“成功即幸福”的观念，那才能说她的说法有道理。

蔡美儿本人的父母认为，得个“A-”，说明还不够好，而她也从来没有质疑过。她解释说，中国父母传达给孩子的意思并不是“你一定要得‘A’，否则我就不喜欢你”。与此相反，他们的意思是：“我特别相信你，我觉得你能得优。”相信孩子的能力固然没错，但在理论上即使所有孩子都能尽力，结果也不是人人都能得优。

我在加拿大当过28年中学教师。通过某件事我认识到，让孩子感受到老师的关爱很重要。回想起来，对自己的120个学生，至少我会找个机会告诉他们每个人我对他们的看法，或者在他们的作业上写下鼓励的话，比如“我喜欢你，因为……”“当你……的时候，我很欣赏你。”可我从来不让学生做其力所不及的事情。相反，我的哲学是，“如果你真做不好，没关系。如果你能做好，那我相信你！”不是每个人都应该在班级里当第一。最重要的是，“在你力所能及的条件下争取最好。”

Desks, blackboards and textbooks? It's not Montessori

An article recently published on *China Daily* about Montessori schools in China led me to write the following considerations.

Ten years ago, a Chinese friend told me his daughter was attending pre-school class at a Montessori school, his eyes inviting me to show approbation and admiration. I was very surprised, since they lived in a disadvantaged region of northwestern China. The little girl had the bad habit to shout her lungs out anytime she spoke, laugh loudly, listen to TV at high volume, slam the doors, etc. She was the absolute contrary of a child modeled by Montessori's theory. I asked the father what he knew about Montessori's philosophy of education; he said that the children "not only learned academic subjects in class but had some time to play freely."

Maria Montessori, born in 1870 in the Italian province of Ancona, became one of the first women doctors in Italy. She worked at a psychiatric clinic, and later, as the director of a school for mentally-disabled children, she observed the children and developed a method which, in two years, brought them to the level of normal children. Encouraged by such success, Dr. Montessori wondered what children with normal potential could do. She returned to school to study anthropology and psychology, and in 1907, was given charge of 50 children from the shanty San Lorenzo district of Rome.

Her theory is based on the spirit of work and peace. She believes that children educate themselves though their work – which is "play". About the principle of independence, Montessori said: "Never help

蒙台梭利教育理念的真谛

最近，《中国日报》发表的一篇关于中国蒙台梭利学校的文章，引发我的一些思考。

10 年前，一个中国朋友告诉我，他的女儿在上一个蒙台梭利学校的学前班。他的眼神期待着我的赞许和羡慕，我听到后感到非常吃惊。他家住在中国西北贫困地区。他女儿说话的时候恨不得把嗓子喊破，笑起来恨不得让所有人都听到，看电视的时候把声音调得很高，出来进去把门摔得山响。她绝对是蒙台梭利学校培养出来的孩子的反面典型。我问孩子爸爸对蒙台梭利的教育理念有什么了解。他说："不但让孩子在课堂学到文化，而且有时间随便玩。"

玛丽亚·蒙台梭利于 1870 年出生在意大利的安科纳省，是意大利的首批女医生之一。她先在一家心理医院工作，后来在担任智障儿童学校校长的时候，她通过观察儿童，发展出了一套自己的教学方法。在两年的时间里，便把智障儿童提高到了正常儿童的水平。成功的实践鼓励启发了蒙台梭利：相对于智障儿童，正常儿童又会有什么样的发展呢？她重返校园，学习人类学和心理学。1907 年，她被委派到罗马圣洛伦佐贫民区，负责 50 名儿童的教学。

她的理论建立在格致与平和精神之上。她相信，儿童可以通过做事，也就是游戏，得到自我教育。对于培养自立，蒙台梭利说："如果孩子

a child with a task he feels he can perform." Teachers, in Montessori classes, don't teach; they guide. Children are the masters; teachers, their servants. Guiding a child means observing and following him. Teachers spend hours only watching children and see how they enjoy themselves and how they explore their environment. When observing the children, they discover how to help them to develop and where they need to be challenged. The aim of "children at work" (playing) is certainly not to learn, but they learn, and often more rapidly than those who are taught language, calculation, art and science the standard way.

"All kinds of learning – musical, bodily-kinesthetic, spatial, interpersonal, intrapersonal, intuitive, natural, and the traditional linguistic and logical-mathematical – are nurtured and respected," said a web source. Children are not taught; they learn independently.

Children don't progress under overprotective parents and adults who always tell them what to do. In a Montessori class, if a child wants to climb, he will be offered, without a word, an opportunity to climb safely. If he starts banging on objects, he will be given a drum; if he pushes things around the room, a wagon to push. According to the child's actions, different materials and toys will be presented to him. But not too much, which would be worse than too little. It is also important that materials are chosen only by experienced teachers.

Children develop their own skills at their own pace, what Montessori calls "spontaneous self-development." Teachers intervene only when children become destructive, waste effort, or develop wrong habits. Children must be able to move freely around the room. "Seldom will two or more children be studying the same thing at the same time. Children learn directly from the environment, and from other children. Teachers care for one child at a time, and almost no lessons are given to the whole class.

觉得能够完成一项任务，老师就不要去帮助他。”在蒙台梭利的班上，老师不教，而是指导。孩子们是主人，老师是他们的仆人。所谓指导孩子，是要求观察学生，随着他们而行动。老师要花很长时间去观察孩子们，看他们如何自得其乐，如何探索周围的一切。老师通过观察，去获得帮助孩子们发展的办法，了解在什么地方需要给他们挑战。“让孩子们做事（玩）”，其目的不是让他们学什么，但是他们从中可以学到东西，而且比用常规的方法教学语言、算术、艺术和科学更见效。

一个网站介绍说：“在这种学校里，各种各样的学习方式——音乐的、身体的、空间的、人际的、内心的、本能的、自然的以及传统的语言和逻辑、数学的方式都能够得到鼓励和尊重。”孩子们不用教导怎样学习，他们在独立学习。

如果家长和成人总告诉孩子做这做那，儿童不会有多大进步。在蒙台梭利学习班里，如果小孩子要爬高，就给他一个安全爬高的机会。如果他开始敲打，就给他一个鼓。如果他推着东西满屋绕，就给他一个小推车。根据孩子活动的不同，给他们提供不同的材料和玩具。但是不要给太多，过犹不及，甚至会更糟。重要的是，要由有经验的老师来为他们挑选所用的材料。

儿童要按照自己的程度发展其技能。蒙台梭利把这个叫作“自发性自我发展”。只有在儿童变得具有破坏性，开始做无用功，或者开始出现坏习惯的情况下，老师才来干预。在教室里，儿童们必须能够自由活动。“很少有两个以上的孩子同时学习同样的东西。孩子们直接从环境学习，从别的孩子那里学习。在一个特定的时间，老师只关照一个孩子。几乎没有给全班上课的时候。”

All children make mistakes. Do they need punishment? Let's say a child drops his glass of milk. The teacher, as well as the parents at home, should say: "Oh! Let's wipe that up together." Never raise your voice; never put the child away from the scene but involve him in the practical action of cleaning. Children's mistakes are not due to misconduct but to something they have not realized. They need to be showed calmly and kindly, otherwise, they will develop fear of being reproached and punished and will not develop their potential.

A prepared environment is essential to physical, intellectual or spiritual results in education. Children need freedom to explore, and the environment must be safe for them to do so. It also has to be calm and beautiful. In a prepared environment, the real world will come out of the child's fertile imagination; he will learn everything without knowing he is learning.

One can see that a non-Montessori-trained teacher can't be expected to teach a Montessori class. During training, the future teachers "practice the many basic lessons with materials in all areas. They must pass difficult written and oral exams on these lessons in order to be certified." Using Montessori's method is extremely challenging, but also rewarding. Now, how many teachers have the needed preparation for teaching in the "300 Chinese and internationally owned kindergartens in Beijing [that] use the Montessori methods"?

Reading the *China Daily* article, I realized that not only the name "Montessori kindergartens" was used to designate all kinds of Western-style preschools, but that Montessori's theory was unknown, misused, and degraded. The article also mentioned "the choice of textbooks" for kindergartens… Montessori kindergartens don't use textbooks. Parents, be aware!

Schools mentioned in the article have 12 to 15 children per class. This

孩子们都会出错，是否需要惩罚呢？比如，当一个孩子把一杯牛奶掉到了地上，学校老师、家里的家长就应该说："来，我们一起把它打扫干净。"永远不要提高嗓门，不要让孩子走开，要让他参与打扫的过程。儿童的错误不是由于故意捣乱造成的，而是由于无知造成的。大人要平静、和蔼地给孩子示范。否则，孩子就会害怕受到责备和惩罚而不敢发展自己的潜能。

教育中，完备的环境对生理、智力和精神各方面的发展都很重要。孩子需要自由探索的空间，他们的环境必须安全。环境的安静和美丽也很重要。良好的环境有助于儿童充分想象真实的世界。他会在不知不觉中学到一切。

由此可见，没有受过蒙台梭利方法训练的老师是不能教好蒙台梭利班的。在训练中，未来的老师们"用各个领域的材料进行基本课程练习。他们必须通过难度很高的考试和面试才能获得证书。"蒙台梭利教学法非常具有挑战性，老师也会有收获。我不禁要问一句："北京300多所使用蒙台梭利方法教学的国内和国际幼儿园，有多少老师已经具备这方面的储备？"

读了《中国日报》的文章，我感觉，中国的"蒙台梭利幼儿园"被当作所有西方式学前教育机构的代称，人们对蒙台梭利的理论或知之甚少，或曲解，或贬低。文章还提到给幼儿园"挑选课本"。家长们要搞清楚：蒙台梭利幼儿园根本不用课本！

该文中提到的学校每个班有12到15个学生。这对一个教"英语、中文、加减法"的中国幼儿园来说很理想。理想的蒙台梭利班有30到

is ideal for a Chinese kindergarten where children are taught "English, Chinese, addition and subtraction." But Montessori ideal classes are of 30-35 children to the same teacher for three years, which "helps to create much independent work, and peers teaching, and eliminates the possibility of too much teacher-centered, teacher-directed work."

After a deep reflection, I sincerely think that Montessori's education is not possible in China. Education doesn't belong to school only. It starts at home, and what is done at school must be corresponded by the family at home. Will Chinese parents, who are used to intervene directly and constantly in their children's wills, decisions, and actions, suddenly change their behavior because their children attend a Montessori school? Can their focus on academic performance change for the valorization of the personality? China is also a country where quietness is unknown. People use their cell phones in public, speak loud in restaurants, on the street and at work, listen to music in their cars and TV at home at high volume; peace – a requirement of Montessori's theory – is nowhere.

* This text appears as an appendix in Carducci, Lisa: *Work in progress - Chinese education from a foreign expert's perspective*, Beijing, China Intercontinental Press, 2012, 190 p.

35 个学生，由同一个老师负责三年，以便“帮助孩子创造独立学习和互相学习的机会，尽量减少教师为主指手划脚的教学活动。”

认真思考后我觉得，蒙台梭利教育法在中国行不通。教育并不局限于学校，学校教育必须有家庭的配合。中国的家长习惯于直接、经常性地干预孩子的意志、决定和行为。难道他们会因为孩子上了蒙台梭利学校而一夜之间改变自己的行为吗？他们会从强调学习成绩变为重视孩子的人格发展吗？中国也是一个不知安静为何物的国家。人们在公共场所使用手机，在餐馆里、大街上和工作场所大声说话，在私家车里大放音乐，在家里把电视调得声音吵人，根本找不到蒙台梭利教育理论所强调的静谧。

* 本文参见 *Work in progress–Chinese education from a foreign expert's perspective* 一书的附录，李莎・卡尔杜齐著，五洲传播出版社，2012 年。

Smell the roses in our Chinese garden

Grass on the other side of the fence is not always greener.

Being a Canadian, I am often asked the best places to immigrate in Canada, with lots of jobs and good salaries, free university, and no food contamination, traffic jams, pollution and corruption.

Is there such a paradise on earth? Twenty years ago, blue skies of Montreal with light white clouds were remarkable; now, we can see the same in Beijing. However, some travelers and residents still confuse fog and pollution.

Caught in a traffic jam in Beijing, my Chinese friends say, "You would never see that in Canada!" The difference is that in Canada, the problem is an old one while it is recent here. Low temperatures of Canadian winter badly damage asphalt roads. China uses concrete instead, but it's too costly for Canadian tax payers who have been squeezed enough. Roads are continuously under repair, to the great annoyance of users.

A Vancouver born Chinese girl came back with her parents after 10 years. She finds it easier to play with friends now. "In Beijing, the public transportation system is very convenient, and I can get anywhere on my own."

The number of bus lines and their frequency amaze visitors in Beijing. In Montreal, waiting time for a bus may be 25 min., and 15 for a subway train.

Many Chinese think that schooling is free in Canada. During the compulsory education period, parents have to pay for notebooks, physical education uniform, science laboratory, compulsory extra

墙内开花自有香

篱笆另一边的草并不总是绿的。

我是加拿大人，所以总是有人问我，移民去加拿大，哪个地方最好，那里工作机会多，薪酬高，有免费大学，没有食品污染，没有交通堵塞，没有空气污染，也没有腐败。

地球上有这样的天堂吗？ 20 年前，蒙特利尔的蓝天白云令人赞叹。在北京现在也可以看到这些，可是有些游客和北京的居民仍然分不清雾和污染。

遇到堵车，我的中国朋友会说："你在加拿大永远不会看到这些！"可是两地区别在于，堵车在加拿大是个老问题了，而在中国却是新问题。加拿大冬天的低温会严重损坏沥青路面，而中国用的是水泥。但这对本已税负很重的加拿大纳税人来说，造价太高。所以，那里的路总是在修啊修，很是扰民。

一个出生在温哥华的中国女孩 10 年后随父母回国。她发现在中国更容易找到朋友。"北京公共交通非常方便。我自己想去哪儿就去哪儿。"

北京公交线路之多，运行之频繁，让来北京的游客感到惊奇。在蒙特利尔，等公车的时间是 25 分钟，地铁是 15 分钟。

很多中国人以为，在加拿大上学是免费的。其实，在义务教育阶段，父母要出钱买笔记本，买体育课的服装，支付实验室的使用费，参加课外活动要额外付费，还要购买保险等。在义务教育阶段之后，学生需要

educational activities, insurances, etc. At a higher level, students often share small apartments in town, and almost all of them work part-time to make is possible to cover their tuition fees, expensive textbooks, student association membership, public transportation fees, etc.

Several Chinese friends ask me whether they should abandon their stable jobs and hard-earned apartments for a new country. My advice is "No". Chances to find the proper job in one's field, well paid, with convenient location, are too low to risk it all.

Canada welcomes mostly political refugees, students with financial support, big investors (a way to fight the high rate of unemployment), and highly qualified persons needed in specific fields. A Chinese scientist heading to Toronto was offered a post in Calgary, a city newly populated by Chinese immigrants. Once there, he was sent to a remote area where his best companions were "cold" and where he felt lonely. He is looking forward to coming back at the end of the two-year project.

New immigrants need time before they are inserted in political and social life. Scandals like ministers owning castles; pet food made from rotten meat; corruption in the building industry; nomination of judges; financing of political parties; poor health of forests, all this remain unknown to several immigrants.

The worsening shortage of "family doctors" is probably unknown too. Doctors all have their quota and one out of seven Quebec citizens is unable to find one. Patients can only wait in emergency halls, and sometimes, late at night, they return home without having seen a doctor.

In that country where human rights are a priority, several homeless elderly and teenagers live on the streets. Defenders of animal rights can't do miracles when a veterinarian charges 2,000 dollars for a problem with a guinea pig's teeth. "I had no choice," said a Chinese

在城里合租小公寓。几乎所有学生都要勤工俭学挣钱，支付学费、不菲的课本费、学生社团费、交通费等。

一些中国朋友问我，是否应该放弃国内稳定的工作和单位分配的住房到国外去生活。我不建议这么做。在国外，能够找到专业对口、薪酬好、工作地点方便的机会很低，不值得去冒这个险。

在加拿大，受欢迎的是政治避难者、有经济来源的学生、大投资商（这是为了对付很高的失业率），以及某些领域的高级专门人才。一个中国科学家移民去了多伦多，却只在卡尔加里找到一份工作，最近这个城市有很多中国移民。他到达后被派到一个偏远的地方，陪伴他的只有寒冷和孤独。他现在盼着两年项目结束后回来。

新移民要融入当地的政治和社会生活需要时间。对于那里发生的丑闻，诸如部长拥有城堡，用腐肉制作宠物食品，建筑业腐败丛生，法官提名黑幕，向政党献金，森林病害等，许多移民都一无所知。

对加拿大存在的“家庭医生”日益缺乏的问题，人们其实也不甚了解。一个医生能收治的病人是有限的。每七个魁北克人中，就有一个找不到家庭医生。病人们只能等在急诊大厅。有的时候，他们等到半夜也没有医生给他们看病，只好回家。

在那个重视人权的国度，却有无家可归的老人和少年露宿街头。为一只宠物猪治疗牙病，兽医开价就 2000 加元。面对这种情况，动物权利保护人士也无法创造奇迹。一个中国父亲说：“无奈之下我把女儿的

father, "but hand my daughter's guinea pig to the SPCA. I felt like a criminal, but how could I pay that amount while a lot of African children die from starvation."

Instead of dreaming of paradise abroad, why not appreciate the huge progress China has accomplished, and continue to help this country develop?

宠物猪交给动物救助组织。这样做让我觉得自己像是犯了罪，但非洲有那么多孩子死于饥饿，我怎么可以把那么多钱花在一只宠物上？”

那些做梦去国外天堂的人，为什么不珍惜中国取得的巨大进步，并继续致力于本国的发展？

Is overseas study boom hurting China's schools?

Many students in China see a degree from an overseas university as the key to a better career back home. Instead, families should start investing and encouraging reform of schools in their own communities.

Each year, hundreds of thousands of Chinese students pursue degrees overseas, especially in Japan, Europe, North America, Australia, and Hong Kong. Nowadays, overseas study is even becoming popular at the undergraduate, secondary and primary school levels.

The boom in overseas study has been attributed to a negative attitude towards the Chinese education system among urban families. According to a 2008 survey of 3,555 Chinese urban residents by the Horizon Research Consultancy Group, 40 percent thought the quality of education in China was not worth the cost. In addition, only 16 percent believed investing in an education in China provided good returns.

A potentially dangerous trend is the increasing number of students who opt out of National Higher Education Entrance Exam, known as the *gaokao*, in order to pursue an overseas study track. In 2009, 10 percent of high-school graduates decided not sit for the exam, and the number has grown for the last three consecutive years. At the end of 2010, a record 1.27 million Chinese were studying abroad, according to the Ministry of Education.

Experts are undoubtedly worried about the "brain exodus" occurring from the Chinese education system, and how it will affect the modernization of China's schools in the long run.

留学海外与立足本土

许多中国学生把外国大学的学位看作回国后获得更好职业的敲门砖。在我看来，家长们应该在本国进行教育投资，并努力促进学校改革。

每年有成千上万的中国学生到海外求学，特别是到日本、欧洲、北美、澳大利亚和香港。如今，本科阶段乃至中小学出国留学也日益盛行。

有观点认为，出国留学人数上升归因于城市居民对中国教育体制的不满。据零点调查集团 2008 年对 3555 个城市居民的调查，有 40% 的人认为，中国的教育质量不值得他们投资。只有 16% 的人认为，投资于中国教育能够得到好的回报。

有一种潜在的危险趋势，越来越多的学生放弃高考，谋求到海外留学。2009 年，决定不参加高考的高中毕业生占到 10%，这一比例过去三年里连续上升。教育部统计，截至 2010 年底，在国外留学人数达到 127 万。

对中国教育系统的“人才流失”，及其对中国学校现代化的长期影响，专家们确实感到担忧。

导致学生离开中国的原因之一是，中国国营和私营企业给予海外学校毕业生的优厚薪酬。另外，国外学历带来的优越感和社会地位的提高也在吸引着他们。

Students are lured away from attending Chinese schools because of the superior financial rewards that state and private enterprises in China offer for graduates of overseas schools. Also they are attracted by the prestige and increased social status that an overseas degree brings.

China is the world's biggest exporter of students. Over 15 percent of international students worldwide come from China, making the country the world's largest economic contributor to the foreign education industry.

Overseas schools offer students educational advantages that are still missing in China. Using scientific methodology, teachers engage students' creativity and critical thinking skills, encourage learning through practice and discovery, and support students' mental, spiritual and physical development. There is also a greater emphasis on extracurricular activities compared to Chinese universities.

Despite the benefits of an overseas education, earning a degree abroad is not always the best choice for students. Some Chinese students face problems adapting to foreign languages and cultures.

"Many young Chinese students are simply unable to adapt to living in a foreign country," said Zhou Zhicheng, a professor who studied in Canada. "Most parents don't know anything about the education structure in other countries, he added. "They just send their children on an adventure."

In addition, families run the risk of being cheated on quality and cost from institutions looking to cash in on the foreign student boom.

"In some cases, a school's marketing department creates a prestigious aura that helps sell the school in China," said Julian R. Taplin, a retired American psychologist. "There can be no doubts that schools short of money are finding the Chinese full-fee market a lifesaver."

In addition to the proliferation of marketing campaigns from overseas schools in the Chinese market, the schools' reputations are also being overinflated at home. A large contingency of local Chinese agencies make a living from fees they charge to students and on commissions they receive from schools for successful placement. As

中国是世界上最大的留学生出口国。全世界留学生中，15% 以上来自中国，这使得中国成为对外国教育产业贡献最大的国家。

外国学校所具有的教育优势在中国还很欠缺。国外老师们用科学的方法激发学生的创造力和批判性思维，鼓励学生们通过实践和发现进行学习，促进学生在脑力上、精神上和体质上的发展。跟中国的大学相比，外国大学更多地强调课外活动。

尽管海外学历有诸多好处，拿到外国学历并不总是学生的最好选择。有的中国学生面临如何适应外国语言和文化的问题。

曾经留学加拿大的周志成教授说："很多年轻的中国留学生根本不能适应国外生活。大部分中国家长不了解其他国家的教育体制。他们其实把孩子送上了一条冒险之路。"

另外，一些学校利用留学热进行赚钱。这也使得一些家庭面临受骗上当的风险，花钱买不到好教育。

已退休的美国心理学家朱利安·R·塔普林说："在某种情况下，学校招生部门会营造出美丽的光环，以促进在中国的推广活动。一些资金短缺的学校无疑会发现中国市场是一个救生圈。"

除了海外学校在中国大力开展的推销活动，这些学校的名声也在中国被吹得神乎其神。中国有一大批的留学中介，他们的生意就是向学生收取介绍费和吃海外学校的回扣。其结果是，并不总是最好或者货真

a result, students who use these services may be matched to a school that is not necessarily the best choice for them or the best value. Agents also downplay the difficulty of successfully completing a degree overseas in order to maximize their own profits.

In 2007, *China Daily* reported that foreign students – mostly Asians – who graduated from Australian universities "have such poor English skills they should never have been admitted," and "more than 43 percent of Chinese graduates don't have sufficient English to work professionally in Australia." The study suggests overseas schools' admissions criteria for international students may play second fiddle to their desire for money.

The current gaps in quality and reputation between Chinese and overseas schools will never be narrowed if education reform in China is not given a chance. Top domestic institutions like Peking University, Tsinghua University, and Fudan University need to take the lead in these modernization efforts.

Nanfang University of Science and Technology in Shenzhen is currently conducting a bold new experiment that could change the face of education in China. The university has no affiliation with China's Ministry of Education. According to Professor Zhu Qingshi, who initiated the experiment, this has allowed the school to cut through red tape and focus on academic quality. 45 brave students are currently studying at the school and will complete their degrees in 2015. Despite the risks, the school says it remains committed to pursuing educational reform.

Reform must start somewhere. Courageous experiments such as Professor Zhu's must be accepted and pushed forward.

价实的学校被介绍给这些接受中介服务的学生。中介机构为了利润最大化，也把读海外学位描述得易如反掌。

2007 年，《中国日报》报道，澳大利亚大学毕业的外国学生大部分是亚洲人，“他们英文之糟糕，从一开始就不应该被录取”，“43% 以上的中国学生的英文能力不足以在澳大利亚从事专业工作。”这项研究认为，外国学校录取留学生的标准可能受到了赚钱欲望的支配。

如果中国不进行教育改革，中国学校和外国学校在质量和名声上的差距将不会缩小。国内知名大学，像北大、清华和复旦应该带头进行现代化改革。

深圳的南方科技大学正在进行可能会改变中国教育面貌的大胆试验，这所大学不属于国家教育部。推动这项试验的朱清时教授说，这可使该校脱离官僚体制的繁文缛节，集中精力提高学术质量。目前就读该校的 45 名学生勇气可嘉，他们将于 2015 年完成学业。校方表示，尽管有各种风险，教育改革的方向不会偏离。

改革总要有个突破口。朱教授的试验应当接受并加以推广。

Do you return home for Xmas?

I remember in the mid-1990s, my Chinese colleagues would leave the office on Dec 24 earlier than normal with a "Merry Xmas, Lisa!", while I used to work till 20:00 to be able to enjoy a day off on Christmas. They used to leave early to celebrate Christmas Eve in a big hotel, with a banquet, dance and all the other trappings.

Those days, Chinese students would offer a card as a gift to their foreign teachers. But nowadays, many young Chinese stick a big Santa Claus on their door, and it remains there for months if not the whole year. Only last month, I told my neighbor in lighter vein: "You better remove that image, or this year Santa Claus will not bring you any gift!" He took it seriously.

Children in kindergartens draw Christmas trees for decoration at school and at home, and many Chinese people have even developed the habit of exchanging gifts of all kinds with their friends.

When I ask my Chinese friends "what and why" they celebrate, they say the Chinese never miss an opportunity to eat and have fun in good company. Why not on Xmas then?

In return, they ask: Do you go back home "*during the merry Xmas*?" as if Xmas was a period, like Spring Festival, which lasts 15 days. As for the word "merry", it is not often used except followed by Xmas.

We Italians have a saying: *Natale con i tuoi, e Pasqua dove vuoi*, meaning that a family reunion is expected on Christmas, but you can celebrate Easter wherever you want. For us, too, Christmas Eve

要回家过圣诞吗?

记得上个世纪 90 年代中期，我的中国同事在 12 月 24 号都提前离开办公室，离开的时候对我说 :“李莎，圣诞快乐！”而我呢，则要工作到晚上 8 点，以便第二天休一天假。中国同事提前下班是为了到一个大宾馆庆祝圣诞夜，包括享用大餐和参加舞会等。

那时候，中国学生一般都给他们的外国老师送一张圣诞卡。可是现在，很多年轻人会把一个很大的圣诞老人贴在门上，而且保留几个月甚至一年。上个月,我半开玩笑地对邻居说:“你最好把那张圣诞老人拿掉，否则今年圣诞老人就不会给你送礼物哦。”他还认真了，赶紧拿掉了。

幼儿园的孩子们画圣诞树装饰教室和家里的墙壁。很多中国人也逐渐习惯朋友之间互送圣诞礼物。

我问中国朋友他们为什么庆祝，庆祝什么，他们说，中国人不想错过在一起吃喝取乐的机会。为什么不趁圣诞玩一玩呢?

他们反过来问我，“快乐（Merry）圣诞期间”你回家吗? 在他们看来，就像 15 天的的春节假期一样，圣诞是个持续很长的节日。他们问话中提到“Merry”(快乐)这个词,如果不是跟 Xmas(圣诞节)一起用，其实是很少使用的。

意大利有句俗语:“圣诞应该在家里过，复活节在哪里庆祝都可以。”我们的圣诞夜也比 25 号这一天重要。圣诞家宴一般有 12 个或 15 个菜，

dinner, comprising 12 or 15 fish and other seafood dishes, is more important than the day of the 25th, a day during which people who have eaten and drunk, and/or narrated stories or played cards all night prefer to rest or sleep.

The Chinese, for sure, know about the link between Christmas and the American roast turkey, but many of them misunderstand that the whole Western world has the same tradition. Many also think Santa Claus belongs to all Western cultures, which, of course, is not true. Italians, for example, have *La Befana*, a witch who distributes gifts (traditionally an orange) to good children and a piece of coal to the bad ones on Jan 6.

Also, very few Chinese know that the Orthodox (who set the date according to the Julian calendar) celebrate Jesus' Nativity on Jan 7. Well, it is not their fault, for even most Westerners don't know that the figure of Santa Claus as we know it today is an American creation of Coca-Cola in 1931.

In fact, Chinese youths who celebrate Christmas in a spirit of love and friendship are reviving the true sense of this festival, while very few Americans I know still honor these values.

But how strange is it that an increasing number of Chinese find *Chun Jie* (Spring Festival) boring? Young girls returning home for family reunions and festivities are afraid of gaining weight because of the sumptuous dinners. Cracking roasted seeds while watching the New Year 4-hour TV show is something youngsters consider annoying and the social gatherings during the period, tedious.

If they prefer Christmas, it is only because it's new to them. People in the countryside don't celebrate it. The youths of the new generation stay in big cities where they work and where there are lots of bars and restaurants. Most of all, they are free to do what they want instead of following traditions. Many say that Western celebrations are more romantic.

有鱼和其他海鲜。圣诞夜酒足饭饱，讲完故事，打过扑克之后，在 25 号这天大家都宁愿好好休息或者睡大觉。

中国人当然知道圣诞节和美国烤火鸡的联系，但是他们很多人误认为西方世界的圣诞传统都一样，以为西方各种文化都有圣诞老人。这当然不正确，比如，意大利还有白发魔女，她在 1 月 6 号给好孩子发礼物（通常是一个橘子），给坏孩子一块煤。

而且，中国人很少知道使用儒略历的东正教在 1 月 7 号庆祝耶稣诞生。但这不怪中国人，因为即使大部分西方人也不知道大家所熟知的圣诞老人只不过是可口可乐公司于 1931 年创造的。

中国青年赋予圣诞节爱和友谊的内涵，其实这代表了节日的真正意义，而我认识的美国人中，很少有人尊崇这些价值观。

但奇怪的是，现在越来越多的中国人觉得春节非常乏味。回家与亲人团聚过年的年轻女孩子害怕丰盛的年夜饭会让她们发胖。年轻人觉得一边嗑瓜子一边看四个小时的春晚很烦人，春节期间的朋友聚会则既累人又无聊。

部分中国人喜欢过圣诞节，那是因为这个节日对他们来说很新鲜。农村人不过圣诞节，年轻人留在自己工作的城市里，那里有很多酒吧和饭馆。更重要的是，他们很自由，可以随心所欲，而不需要遵从什么传统。很多人说西式的庆祝活动更为浪漫。

Young couples are often taken up by their professional obligations and cite one excuse or another not to go back home for Spring Festival. Some send their children alone to their grandparents while they stay behind in cities to entertain their customers and develop their business relationships.

Do young Europeans follow their traditions? Not all of them. But since Christmas is only a one-day affair, it's easier for them to sacrifice 24 hours rather than two weeks Spring Festival requires.

Last year I heard that some Chinese are trying to spread *Chun Jie* celebrations among non-Chinese people abroad. Trying to popularize Chinese celebrations among Westerners may not be such a good idea. For me, it is as "strange" as for the non-Christian Chinese to celebrate Xmas. Why not celebrate the Muslim and the Jewish festivals then? But it's a treat to watch Chinese overseas communities celebrate their festival, with lion dance and fireworks, publicly. And sharing happiness is not a bad thing, right?

年轻的夫妇常常因为工作而要留在城市，他们找借口不回老家过年。有的把孩子送到爷爷奶奶那里，而自己则留在城里接待客户，拓展生意。

欧洲的年轻人是否按传统习俗过节呢？也不全是。然而，圣诞节只不过一天时间，他们牺牲 24 个小时比春节的两个星期更容易做到。

去年，我听说有些中国人试图把春节庆祝活动推广到海外非华人中去。在西方人中推广春节可能不是一个好主意。对我来说，这就跟让非基督徒的中国人庆祝圣诞节一样“奇怪”。那为什么不能庆祝穆斯林和犹太人的节日？不过，看海外华人为庆祝春节而进行的舞狮表演和放烟花，也是一件赏心悦目的事。分享幸福不是一件坏事，对吧？

About translation

As a linguist, and as a Canadian, a country where one of the two official languages (English and French) is in danger, I would like to express my concern about Chinese language also. Some Chinese scholars insist on the importance of taking measures to avoid Chinese language mingling with English. They are right, this is important. But the solution is not translating all foreign words comprised in Chinese texts.

Foreign words used in Chinese must be classified in different categories. When talking about abbreviations including CEO, GPD, WTO and CPI, those that designate Chinese realities should be replaced by typically Chinese expressions which are clear for the users.

My view is different regarding individual and topographic names, as well as foreign companies, products and organizations names.

For instance, the "ka" syllable of Canada, Canon, and Carducci have been translated into Chinese as 加, 佳, and卡, respectively meaning "to add", "excellent", and "card"; only the third one reproduces the exact pronunciation. For the Chinese, the meaning of a character and its beauty prevail on its sound to the point that it is often impossible to imagine, from its Chinese translation, what the original name was. The Italian name Antonio is translated 安东尼奥 "An dong niao", or worse, as an English name, 安东尼 (Anthony), "because we don't use *tou* in names", said a Chinese translator, as they are usually very complicated or they have negative meaning. With so many Chinese characters pronounced "tou", I hardly believe there is no one acceptable!

谈翻译

作为一个来自有英语和法语两种官方语言的加拿大的语言文字工作者，我想说说我对中文使用情况的担心。中国有些学者非常强调不能在中文中混杂英语，他们的观点很正确，这一点很重要。但是，解决的办法并不是要把所有的外文词语翻译过来。

对中文中的外文词语应该分类对待。对于 CEO、GDP、WTO 和 CPI 等缩略语，以及那些表示中国事物的名词，应该用使用者能够明白的中文词语代替。

对于人名、地名、外国公司和组织名称的翻译，我有不同的看法。

例如，在 Canada, Canon, Carducci 这些词里的“ka”音，中文翻译成“加、佳和卡”。这三个字的意思分别是“增加”、“很好”和“卡片”。只有第三个字正确反映了“ka”的读音。在翻译中，中国人讲究达意形美胜过发音。很多专有名词，从中文翻译无法追溯其原文。意大利人名“Antonio”被翻译成“安东尼奥”，甚至翻译成英文的“安东尼”（Anthony）。一个中国翻译说，我们在人名里不用发音为“tou”的字，这些字不是很复杂就是意思不好。我不明白：中文里发音为“tou”的字那么多，难道就没有适合翻译人名的吗？

Another example: who can guess YashiLandai (雅诗兰黛) is the famous Estée Lauder? Phonetically, it could have been translated 爱斯提・劳德, with these or other good-looking and good-meaning characters, and the pronunciation would have been much closer to the original. Saying this, I am aware that my proposal would never be accepted as a translation for the brand name, as the concern "is not" to be able to recognize the original name, as I wish it would, but to create a Chinese name which can help marketing the product. For a cosmetic producer, 雅诗兰黛 is not a bad choice, indeed, as the characters refer to "elegance", "poetry", and colors reminding the kohl women used to embellish their eyes. And 黛 is the character used for Lin Daiyu, the main figure of Dream of the Red Chamber.

When a Chinese talks with a non-Chinese and mentions "Limadou", even a foreigner who speaks perfect Chinese can't guess this means Matteo Ricci. A Chinese translator will object that 利玛窦 is a historical translation, and the Chinese translation circle does not favor making a new translation.

But names of foreign actors in film cast and artists in museums – recently translated – often become unrecognizable.

That is why we should also preserve the original names in Latin alphabet in a text. If a Chinese goes on line to deepen his research about 雅诗兰黛 or 利玛窦, he will have access to Chinese information only, as he doesn't know the names in their original languages.

Recently I was talking with a Buddhist lama and mentioned "Mandala". He didn't know this Sanskrit word – which is basic in Buddhism – and I didn't know it in Chinese. A large number of languages which use Latin alphabet set one spelling for foreign words, the closest to the original pronunciation, and they all use the same word, such as "spaghetti" (Italian), "tennis" (English), "fuhrer" (German), "corrida" (Spanish), "veranda" (Portuguese), "pacha"

另外一个例子是“雅诗兰黛”。你能想象得到那就是有名的“Estée Lauder”品牌的翻译？按照发音，这个名称本来可以翻译成“爱斯提·劳德”，其中没有形、意不好的字，且发音则更加接近原文。其实，我并非不知道这个译法不可能被采纳，因为品牌译名注重的不是我所在乎的能否追溯原文，而是能否推销产品。对于一个美容产品来说，这个译名体现优雅诗情、兰黛横波，况且又用到了《红楼梦》中林黛玉名字中的“黛”，“雅诗兰黛”的确是一个不坏的选择。

中国人跟外国人聊天，说起“利玛窦”，就是中文很好的老外也猜不出那就是“Matteo Ricci”。这个名字没有别的翻译，因为中国译者会说那是一个颇有历史的译名，翻译界不愿另造一个译名。

但问题是新近翻译的电影里的外国演员以及博物馆里的外国艺术家的名字，也难以分辨。

所以，我们应该在文章中保留这些名称的拉丁拼写。如果一个中国人上网查找有关雅诗兰黛或者利玛窦的资料，他只能查到中文的，因为他不知道其外文原名。

最近，我跟一个喇嘛提起“Mandala ”（曼陀罗）。他不知道这个佛教里的基本梵语词语，我也不知道中文怎么翻译。很多使用拉丁字母的语言处理外来词语的时候，都使用最接近原文发音的拼法并且保持始终，比如 spaghetti（意大利语）、tennis（英语）、fuhrer（德语）、corrida（西班牙语）、veranda（葡萄牙语）、pacha（土耳其语）、Islam（阿拉伯语）、

(Turkish), "Islam" (Arabic), "geyser" (Icelandic), "Inuit" (Eskimo), etc., what is a very pragmatic choice. Chinese are obsessive sticklers for translation.

Some Chinese realities can't and must not be translated. "Jiaozi" should remain jiaozi in other languages; they are not at all "raviolis". French, English speakers, etc. use the Italian word "ravioli" because they eat Italian raviolis. They didn't translate the word into their language because there is nothing equivalent to raviolis in their own culture.

When adapting an alphabetic language (Latin, Cyrillic, Arabic) into a non-alphabetic language such as Chinese, a whole syllable must be converted into a single character. In this situation, it's essential that the character is chosen accordingly to the original pronunciation. Francesco (Italian) and Francisco (Spanish) should be written differently in Chinese (which is not the case). And Napoli and Venezia should have been translated from the original Italian (na-po-li, wei-nei-zi-ya), not from the English Naples (Nabulesi) and Venice (Weinise).

As there is a Dictionary for translating foreign proper names – a professional reference book – to prevent translators from inventing their own translations, no space is left for correction and improvement.

When Beijing subway line 4 opened, I discovered that the well-known Hailong electronic market in Zhongguancun had become Hilon market. Hailong means "Sea Dragon" in Chinese, a beautiful and powerful image. Even those who don't know Chinese can pronounce correctly Hailong. What was the reason to change it into Hilon, a word without meaning and more difficult to remember?

geyser（冰岛语）、Inuit（爱斯基摩语），等等。这种方法很实用，但中国人非要进行翻译。

中国的有些事物不能而且不该翻译。饺子就应该是“jiaozi”，而不应该是“raviolis”（一种意大利面食，包有奶酪等，类似馄饨。）。法语、英语中均使用意大利语“ravioli”这个词，因为他们吃这种食物。他们没有把这种食物翻译成法语和英语,因为在他们的文化中没有这种食品。

从拼音文字（拉丁文、斯拉夫文、阿拉伯文）向诸如中文这样的非拼音语言转换时，一个音节应该对应于一个汉字。重要的是，汉字的发音要对应于原文的发音。意大利语的“Francesco”和西班牙语的“Francisco”在中文里的译法应该不同（实际情况并非如此）。“Napoli”和“Venezia”应该按照意大利语的发音翻译成“那波利”和“威内西亚”，而不应该从英文翻译为“那不勒斯”和“威尼斯”。

由于有专门的译名词典之类的参考书，译者避免自创译名，就没有进一步修正。

北京的地铁 4 号线开通后，我发现海淀区的“海龙电子城”变成了“Hilon 市场”。原来的名字是“海中之龙”的意思，很美、很给力。不会中文的人也能正确读出“hailong”的发音。为什么改成“Hilon”这样一个毫无意义而且难于记忆的词?

As a linguist with 20-year experience in Chinese translation versus French, English and Italian, I would recommend two points:

– First, to create a series of characters reserved to the phonetic translation of foreign names (as this exists in Japanese), no matter the meaning of the characters is.

– Second, to keep the original spelling of foreign personal names in Latin alphabet in parenthesis the first time the Chinese translation appears in a text, for instance: 利玛窦 (Matteo Ricci).

作为一位在中文与法文、英文和意大利文翻译方面有 20 多年工作经验的语言工作者，我有两点建议：

第一，创立一批专门用于外国名称音译的汉字（就如日文那样），不牵涉汉字的意义。

第二，首次翻译时，保留外文名称的拼写，并放在括弧里，如利玛窦 (Matteo Ricci)。

Not drunk, but...

When I came to live in China in 1990, I had to give up my daily glass of wine with dinner. Italians in Canada used to make their own wine for the year. In change, Five Stars beer was available for 0,8 yuan a bottle, but I'm not really a beer drinker.

I later found Chinese dry red wine called "*ganhong*", but it was *gan* only on the label. The content was grape juice, mixed with alcohol and sugar. The Chinese who happened to taste "real" wine would add sugar or Sprite to it as they found the taste too sour. Today's Chinese have got used to high quality wine from all over the world and also domestic brands. But the drinking culture still amazes me.

Drinking in China is not aimed at quenching one's thirst. It is a public act with rich social meaning. When foreign guests are invited to a banquet, a drop of red wine in a glass is usually presented, but it must not be touched before the MC proposes a toast. Meanwhile, waiters would ask guests what they prefer: Coca-Cola, milk, yoghurt, or juices from coconut, kiwi, and carrot to jujube, lotus, or almond, which are mostly for women, while beer is offered to men. Tea, as well as *baijiu*, is not meant to wash down a meal. Once I said I would continue with wine, the waiter thought I had not got his question and asked an interpreter to come and solve the "problem".

I soon realized the wisdom of having something else to drink but alcohol because you should drink the wine or spirit at the invitation of another guest who proposes a toast. If you take you glass first, your companions will immediately take theirs, ready to drink after you propose a toast.

谈谈中国的酒文化

1990 年，我来到中国生活，无奈放弃了每日饮用葡萄酒的习惯。加拿大的意大利人通常自己酿酒喝。在中国，五星牌啤酒八毛钱一瓶，不过我并不怎么喝啤酒。

后来，我发现中国有种“干红”葡萄酒，但是这种葡萄酒的“干”只是写在标签上而已。酒的成分是葡萄汁加酒精和糖。中国人喝“真正”的葡萄酒觉得太酸，就会往里面加糖或者“雪碧”饮料。如今中国人已经习惯饮用世界各地高质量的葡萄酒以及本国牌子的葡萄酒，可是中国的饮酒文化仍然让我感到惊奇。

在中国，喝酒并非为了解渴，而是一种有着丰富社会意义的公共活动。外国人应邀出席宴会的时候，都会拿到一杯红酒，但是主持人提议祝酒之前是不能碰的。

我意识到，在宴会上喝饮料而不喝酒，乃是明智之举。因为别人端起酒杯祝酒，你是不能不喝的。如果你先拿起酒杯，你的伙伴们会马上拿起酒杯，等着你祝酒，然后大家一饮而尽。

The hard core of Chinese drinking culture is *baijiu*, liquor with high alcoholic volume, that the Chinese believe only they are strong enough to imbibe. They are always surprised when a non-Chinese can absorb a certain quantity of it, especially a woman.

In 1995, a Chinese magazine invited me and four other Western authors to visit Shandong Province. For health reasons, the two men could not take any alcohol, and the North-European woman had never drunk a drop before.

At the welcoming banquet, our table was separate from our hosts', which gave me the chance to tell the three non-drinkers that they could empty their glasses secretly in a little bowl after each feigned bottom up.

The American woman, who had just come to China, liked the taste of *baijiu* very much and even asked for more. I warned her that each of our six hosts would come to our table to propose a toast, and we would show our gratitude and respect with "*ganbei*". Tiny glasses are used as the content has to be gulped down.

But she didn't mind, took all the toasts and more, and... went to bed. The next day we left for a visit without her, as she couldn't get up.

Chinese attach great importance to drinking. During the lunch with the mayor, I was seated at his right. I felt my responsibility to "save the Westerners' face". For saving face, Chinese would even risk their health to down every cup of liquor at a banquet.

But I did something wrong, though I thought was very clever at first: I filled an empty bottle of *baijiu* with water, and grabbed each chance to refill my glass before the mayor could, but never filled his glass. This was really strange for the Chinese, who regard filling a guest's glass with liquor an expression of respect.

中国饮酒文化中，白酒是一大难关。这种酒烈度很高，中国人认为只有他们才喝得了。他们看到一个外国人，特别是外国女人，能够喝下大量的烈酒时，都会惊奇不已。

1995 年，一家中国杂志邀请我和另外四名西方作家访问山东。其中两位男士由于健康原因不能喝酒，另一位北欧女士从来没沾过一滴酒。

在欢迎宴会上，我们跟主人不在同一张桌子上。这让我有机会告诉我的三个不喝酒的同伴：祝酒的时候，他们只要做做样子，然后把酒偷偷倒在一个碗里就行了。

那位美国女士是第一次到中国，她很喜欢白酒的味道，喝了还要再喝。我警告她说，我们的东道主六个人会一个个地来敬酒，为了表示感谢和尊敬，我们得干杯。用的杯子是小杯，因为必须一口喝干。

可是她不在乎，一杯杯地把敬的酒都喝了。第二天，我们出去参观没带她，因为她起不了床。

中国人很看重饮酒。跟市长共进午餐的时候，我坐在他右边。我也感到自己有责任“为西方人挣面子”。中国人为了面子，在宴会上喝起酒来是不管身体健康的。

可是我还是聪明反被聪明误。开始时我在白酒瓶子里掺了水，不失时机地抢在市长前头给自己斟满酒。对于中国人来说,我的行为很奇怪，为了表示对客人的尊重，他们都是要先给客人斟酒的。

After a dozen toasts, the mayor said between his teeth something like: "That woman is too strong." He grabbed my bottle, smelled it, and ordered the waitress to bring a "genuine" one.

Mea culpa, I had cheated. When the banquet finally ended, my two male colleagues came along, supporting me on either side as I was walking on clouds, under a whirling ceiling. Not drunk, but almost.

喝了十几盅以后，市长嘟囔了一句，好象是说：“这个女人很能喝。”他拿过我的瓶子闻了闻，然后命令服务员拿“真的”来。

结果呢，我是自作自受。宴会好不容易结束了，我的两个男同事走过来，一边一个扶着我走。我就像腾云驾雾一样，觉得天旋地转。我还没醉，不过也差不多了。

My dream of Taiwan

In 2005, I finished my tour of all the provinces, regions and municipalities of China. I had waited for Hong Kong to return to the motherland in 1997, and I also visited Macao after 1999. I was only waiting for Taiwan to reunite with the continent before going there. But, in recent years, the three links with the mainland have been re-established, special flights have been organized across the Strait, and the Chinese living in Beijing, Shanghai and Guangzhou have been authorized to take personal trips to the island. I was tempted to visit Taiwan earlier than expected.

I started reading about Taiwan, and suddenly I remembered that, 18 years ago, I used to have *Taiwan niuroumian* (beef noodles) in a special restaurant in Beijing downtown. But, unfortunately, this restaurant had closed, and I never had the Taiwan dish after that.

My desire grew stronger and stronger to the point that I decided to book with a group of Chinese travelers.

The day before I left Beijing, the *China Daily* reported that a new Taiwan beef noodles restaurant had just opened at Wangfujing. My mouth watered, and I thought how lucky I was: I would have the original noodles on the original land!

Chinese are deeply interested by what they eat. Wherever they travel, they evaluate the countries accordingly to the food: eatable or not. In Taiwan, the first time the local guide addressed us, she spoke about food: "Taiwan dishes are a little sweet… You – from the continent – will find that salt is missing… We don't use *weijing*…" etc.

我的台湾梦

到 2005 年,我已游历完了中国大陆各省、自治区和直辖市。1997 年，我翘首期待香港回归。1999 年后，我又去了澳门。我就等着台湾跟大陆统一后去台湾了。近年来，台湾与大陆实现了三通，包机可以直接飞越台湾海峡了。北京、上海和广州的市民都可以到台湾旅游了，我的台湾游计划禁不住也提前了。

为此，我阅读了相关资料。这让我回忆起 18 年前曾在北京市内一家特色餐馆吃过的台湾牛肉面。遗憾的是，此餐馆后来关张了，我便再也无缘台湾牛肉面。

我的兴致日渐强烈，我决定随旅游团前往。

离京前一日,《中国日报》报道王府井新开了一家台湾牛肉面。此消息令我垂涎，我对自己将在原产地尝到原汁原味的台湾牛肉面感到幸运!

中国人对饮食兴趣甚浓。无论到何处旅游，评价起来往往都以饮食可口与否为参照。在台湾，导游首次介绍台湾便说“台湾饮食偏甜，大陆人士会觉得咸味不足，台湾烹饪不用味精”，等等。

Though we had "group canteen" food, I found it delicious. We had sea food, fish or crab at every meal, different meats, tofu and lots of vegetables. But I longed for *Taiwan niuroumian*, and the third day, I asked the guide when we were going to have some.

Surprised, she said it had not been planned that we had. The next day, we had *hongshaorou* and it reminded me of the jade *hongshaorou* that we had seen at the Imperial Palace Museum. I was dreaming of Taiwan beef noodles.

We had wonderful dishes of meat, fish, vegetables, tropical fruit imported from Hainan or Thailand, and extra such as sweets and *cha jidan* (eggs boiled in tea), but my stomach was not satisfied. I told the guide I would skip one meal and go to fulfil my dream by myself. She said that I would not find noodles in the area, and as the meal time was only 30 min., I had no time to go to such a restaurant far away.

In Gaoxiong, we paid homage to the late singer Deng Lijun (Teresa), and went out to the night market, where, among 100 kinds of Taiwan snacks, I found beef noodles that made me blush: they looked like *fangbianmian* (instant noodles). I was not going to have that for sure. No matter, I said to myself, I will have the delicacy when we go back to the hotel, as I had spotted a small shop selling all kinds of beef noodles. But when I returned it had just closed, and the next morning we were leaving for Zhiben at 7:00.

On the seventh day, a big bowl of noodles was deposited on our table: pre-cooked noodles added to a broth as clear as water. A pale reminiscence of what it should be... I just kept silent.

We were about to end our tour and I had not even smelled the aroma of the Taiwan beef noodles.

I told my travel companions that I had found only one negative aspect during our trip. They smiled with compassion for the "Foolish *laowai* with a dream".

虽然旅行团吃饭方式是“团餐”，食物却很美味。每餐都有鱼或蟹，还有各类肉食、豆腐和青菜，然而我却始终不忘牛肉面。第三天，我问导游何时去吃牛肉面。

导游很吃惊，说旅游计划中并无此项目。次日，我们吃的是红烧肉，不禁令我想起故宫博物院展出的肉形石。不过，我还是念念不忘牛肉面。

餐桌上非常丰盛，有鱼、肉和青菜，海南或泰国的热带水果，甜食和茶鸡蛋，可是我的肠胃还不满足。我告诉导游我要免去一餐，自己去找梦中的台湾牛肉面。她说附近没有面馆，吃饭时间只有 30 分钟，到别处去找时间不够。

在高雄，我们参观了邓丽君纪念馆，然后去了夜市。百余种台湾小吃里，我找到了牛肉面，却大失所望：跟方便面无异，我要吃的显然不是这样的面！我安慰自己说，回到宾馆后我会去品尝我的美食，因为此前已经发现附近一家餐馆有各种牛肉面。岂料，回到宾馆之时，餐馆已经打烊，次日早上七点我们要出发去知本温泉。

第七天，餐桌上添了一大碗面条：清汤里是一团预先煮熟的面，不由得令人去回忆真正的面条究竟该是什么样。我简直无语。

旅行就要结束了，我连牛肉面的香味都没闻到。

我告诉同行旅友，此次观光只有一个美中不足，他们听后莞尔一笑：这个充满梦想的傻老外啊！

The day of departure arrived, and we were driven to Taoyuan Airport. I had to say goodbye to Taiwan without having beef noodles. What a pity! This is what happens when you travel with a group but stick to personal aspirations!

I arrived in Beijing with my dream sticking to me. Two days later, I took a bus to downtown to savour my *Taiwan niuroumian*. But Wangfujing is large, and the *China Daily* article didn't mention the address. I asked nine people on the street and in different stores… Guess what? No one had ever heard of CHEF HUNG NIU ROU MIAN. I came back home angry, and hungry!

返程那天，我们被送往桃园机场。我没有吃到牛肉面，却不得不对台湾说再见，真是遗憾！随团旅游，却心存私愿，结果总会如此！

带着自己的牛肉面之梦，我回到北京。两天以后，乘公交去城里品尝我的台湾牛肉面。王府井很大，《中国日报》没有说那家餐馆在哪里。我在几家餐馆先后问过 9 个人。你猜如何？他们没人听说过“洪师傅牛肉面”。我饥肠辘辘地回到家，满腹怨气！

Relativity is not exclusively Einstein's matter

Spring festival will arrive as early as Jan. 23 in 2012. I'm wondering where I will spend it.

In 2010, I spent the Chinese New Year in Chini, a Tibetan village of Deqing Prefecture in Yunnan at 3,600 m above sea level.

When I say that to my friends, their first reaction is, "It must have been veeery cold!" In fact it was not at all. I left Beijing at -3 °C on Feb 9, and the temperature was 12 °C in Lhasa, capital of the Tibet autonomous region, at the same altitude as Chini.

Some days later, it was 9 °C in Beijing and 23 °C in Lhasa. At such altitudes, it seems that we are so close to the sun that we could touch it. If, inside the house, we have to keep our coats on, we can raise our sleeves outside. It's all relative.

High daytime temperatures don't mean that it never snows. It snowed three nights in a row. The landscape was like a fairytale in the morning, and I took lots of pictures.

However, the family I was visiting had mixed feelings: They were happy because water was desperately needed for the fields, but worried because the date of a wedding in the family was close, and the banquet for more than 100 people would be set on the *qingke* (highland barley) field. The *qingke* grass was already 10 to 15 cm high, but there was no problem to walk and sit on it, they said.

In Montreal, we used to say jokingly that there are two seasons: Winter, and July.

People think that because I was born in Canada, I surely love winter and am used to the cold. Montreal's winters are humid and

这里也有相对论

2012 年的春节（1 月 23 日）快到了。我在想我应该去哪里过春节。

2010 年的春节，我是在云南的德钦县赤尼村过的。那是一个藏族村落，海拔 3600 米。

我告诉朋友们后，他们的第一反应就是“那儿一定非常冷！”其实不然，2 月 9 号，我离开北京的时候，是零下 3 度，跟赤尼同样海拔的西藏拉萨的气温却是零上 12 度。

几天以后,北京气温零上 9 度,而拉萨是零上 23 度。在这样的海拔，我们似乎离太阳很近，触手可及。我们在屋里要穿上大衣，而在外面则可以挽起袖子。一切都是相对的。

白天气温高并不意味着不会下雪，一连三个晚上那里都下了雪。早上起来，外面的景致如同童话中的仙境。我拍了很多照片。

可是，我所访问的家庭对这种天气却喜忧参半，喜的是下雪给他们带来了农田需要的水分，忧的是他们马上要举行一场婚礼，一百多人的婚宴要在青稞地里举行。青稞已经长到 10 到 15 厘米高了，可是他们说踩在上面或者坐在上面都没有问题。

在蒙特利尔，我们常常开玩笑说那里只有两个季节，冬天和七月。

因为我是加拿大出生的，人们总是以为我一定喜欢冬天，一定适应

windy. The best winter days are when it snows, because there is no wind when snowflakes fall, covering the houses, streets and cars under a 1-meter-thick blanket. Snow doesn't mean cold.

This year, I spent the Spring festival with another Tibetan family in Qinghai province's Tongren county.

In Yunnan's Tibetan houses, the fireplace is a square in the soil. Tibetans use wood for cooking and heating, and they sit on the ground on flat cushions or low stools around the fireplace.

In Qinghai, they use an iron stove in the middle of the main room, where the whole family concentrates during the day in winter, while other rooms are closed until the summer. They burn some wood and coal but mostly yak dung, which is odorless and smokeless but burns quite fast.

Every day from 10 am to 3 pm, it was a pleasure to sit outside sewing, chatting or helping the children with their holiday homework – writing diaries in Chinese and in Tibetan. With more than one piece of clothing, I would sweat. How pleasant was it to feel the sun on my arms!

But as soon as the sun disappeared behind the mountain peak, the air became chilly. Inside the house, a coat was needed and hats, scarves and gloves were welcome.

The bedrooms were not heated. I was given the best one, which had a *kang* (a brick bed heated underneath) that I shared with the family's two girls. Under the blanket, I remained warm long enough to fall asleep, although the temperature in the rest of the room was below 0 C. In the morning, I would find my toothpaste, hand cream and the water left in the basin turned into ice.

Back in Beijing, when people saw my suntan, they thought I had spent two weeks on a beach somewhere in the south.

Snowy mountains, winter chills and warm hearts show a different theory of relativity.

了寒冷。蒙特利尔的冬天潮湿而多风。冬天最好的时候是下雪的时候，因为那时候没有风。一米厚的雪毯覆盖了房屋、街道和汽车，下雪并不见得冷。

今年的春节，我是在青海同仁县一个藏民家里过的。

在云南的藏民家里，火塘是地上的一个方形的坑。他们烧木头做饭，围着火塘坐在垫子或者矮凳子上取暖。

在青海，他们在客厅的中间安放一个铁炉子。冬天的时候，全家人的活动都集中在这里。其他房间则关闭到夏天才使用。他们也烧木头和煤，但是大部分时间烧牛粪。牛粪烧起来无烟无味，但是烧得很快。

每天从 10 点到下午 3 点，他们在屋外坐着缝衣服、聊天、帮孩子做作业（用汉文和藏文写日记），很是惬意。如果身上穿几层衣服，我还会出汗。赤裸胳膊晒太阳则感到很舒服！

可是一旦太阳下山，马上冷起来。在屋内，需要穿大衣，最好也戴上帽子、手套和围巾。

卧室没有取暖设备。他们给我安排最好的房间，我跟两个女孩子睡在火炕上。在被子下面，我可以暖暖和和地入睡，而被子外面的室温则在零度以下。早上起来，我的牙膏、护手霜和脸盆里的水全都冻成了冰。

回到北京后，别人看到我脸晒黑了，还以为我在南方的海滩上度过了两个星期。

雪山、寒冬和热心肠诠释了另一种不同的相对论。

A taste for luxury goods

According to a report published by World Luxury Association quoted by *China Daily* on Dec. 26, 2011, "total consumption in the Chinese mainland luxury market reached $10.7 billion in 2010, excluding private jets, yachts or luxury cars, making the country the world's second largest consumer of luxury goods following Japan."

Fake brand-name goods and illegal copies no longer interest the Chinese, but if they buy in Taiwan, they can enjoy a huge tax refund or exemption that easily covers the 5,000 yuan the guided tour costs, which include flights, hotels, three meals a days, air-conditioned bus rides, and admission fees at museums and scenic attractions.

I also learned about Chinese mainlanders while observing them spending without limits – some of them in a compulsive way – on luxury cosmetics and brand-name goods. A woman spent over 20,000 yuan on three handbags. A young couple bought a huge amount of tea packs to give to friends and colleagues. They made me ask myself the questions: Is China still a developing country? What about the gap between the rich and the poor? As the rich get richer, the poor get poorer. In a sane society, isn't such a phenomenon moral?

With the economic development of the country, the Chinese mentality has changed rapidly. In the past, the Chinese were frugal, not because they didn't have money, but because they valued this life attitude. Economy, discipline, sobriety – these Chinese people's precious qualities – are no longer valued as they were not so long ago.

奢侈品之惑

2011 年 12 月 26 日,《中国日报》援引“世界奢侈品协会”的报告说：“2010 年，除了私人飞机、游艇和豪华轿车，中国大陆奢侈品消费总量达到 107 亿美元，使中国成为仅次于日本的世界第二大奢侈品消费国。”

中国人对于仿冒名牌产品和非法的盗版产品已经不感兴趣。如果他们在台湾购买真正的名牌产品，他们可以享受很大幅度的退税或者免税待遇。这足以抵消 5000 元的参团旅游费。这个费用包括来回机票、饭店住宿、一日三餐、空调旅游车和博物馆以及风景点的门票。

我通过观察，对大陆有些人出手阔绰的消费行为也有所了解。他们有些人购买奢侈品和名牌货是不得已而为之。一名妇女花了两万元买了 3 个女用手提包。一对年轻夫妇买了大量的茶送给朋友和同事。他们的行为让我疑惑：中国还是一个发展中国家吗？贫富差距的问题怎么解决呢？富人越来越富，穷人越来越穷。在一个理智的社会里，这种现象合乎道德规范吗？

国家经济的迅速发展，很快改变了中国人的心态。过去，中国人很节俭，这倒不是因为没有钱，而是因为他们崇尚这种生活态度。节俭、自律和朴素，中国人曾经看重的宝贵品质现在不再那么受重视了。

Most of my travelling companions had converted thousands of yuan on arrival, while I had changed only 300 yuan – as all expenses were paid. People around me started to wonder whether I was poor… or even a "spy". So, on the bus, I asked the guide to let me use the microphone to explain to the group of 15 that I did not judge, criticize or blame them. They could do what they want with their honestly earned money. But, my purpose for traveling was different from theirs. I have visited dozens of countries; what I like is discovering the people and the way they live and think. I also told the group what I do with my money: I prefer to support the education of the needy children in China. During the last five years, I have helped several humanistic and cultural projects mainly for the Tibetan communities of Qinghai, with my money and with donations. Fund raising is still very difficult… How great could it be if only 0.5 percent of the money spent on luxury goods could be donated to keep people alive and allow children to go to school?

跟我同团的大多数游客到达台湾后都兑换了上千元人民币，而我只兑换了三百元——旅行团所有的开销都包括进去了，我没有什么别的花销。其他人开始怀疑我是不是很穷，甚至是不是“间谍”。我在车上用导游的话筒对车上15名游客说，我不会评判、批评或者谴责他们。他们用自己诚实的劳动挣来的钱，爱怎么花就怎么花。只是我的旅游的目的跟他们的不同。我去过很多国家，我喜欢了解各地的人民和他们的生活及思维方式。我也告诉他们我自己怎么花钱。我宁可把钱用在帮助贫穷家庭的孩子接受教育上。过去5年里，我自己出钱，或用捐款资助青海藏族社区的文化教育项目。筹款并不那么容易，如果能把花在奢侈品上的钱拿出千分之五来帮助人们解决生存问题，帮助孩子读书上学，那该多好啊！

Free, safe, and doubly efficient

In December, 2011, Xie Jianping was offered a seat among the elite of the Chinese Academy of Engineering. His election as an academician ignited fierce controversy among the public. The main reason was Xie researches ways to make cigarettes less harmless, instead of means to ban tobacco consumption. Another objection was the institute he works for is affiliated with China National Tobacco Corp., the country's largest tobacco company, and that most of his research is sponsored by the tobacco industry.

One of my hobbies and passion consists in growing all kinds of plants at home. My friends often say, "You have many plants, don't you?" Once I decided to count them. I was astonished to discover 165 pots in four different locations in my apartment including a large, sunny veranda.

As I travel quite often and leave the care of plants to my neighbor, I realized it was too much work for him, and I reduced the number of pots to only 78.

When I offer plants to friends, they usually say: "Give me a piece and I will graft it at home." But this doesn't help me to lower the number of pots. It's the whole pot or nothing!

I also have a bête noire: inhaling the smokers' exhaled poison. At one time, the right to smoke was as strong as the right to live in a sanitary environment. We had no choice but put up with smokers everywhere. So, I used to take my revenge at home – my private territory – and never allowed visitors to smoke in my apartment. If my guests lit a cigarette, I would ask them to extinguish it. But because I had no ashtray, they would usually stub it out in one of the flowerpots.

“院士”助戒烟

2011年12月，谢剑平当选中国工程院院士，在公众中引起强烈质疑。反对的主要原因是，他的研究不是关于怎么戒烟，而是怎样给烟减害。反对的另外一个原因是，他的研究院跟中国烟草公司有关系，而中国烟草公司是全国最大的烟草公司，谢的研究大部分都是烟草工业资助的。

我有很多爱好,其中之一是在家里种各种植物。我的朋友常常说:“你的植物很多，是吧？”有一次我决定数一数，结果却吃惊地发现在我公寓的四个地方，包括一个大阳台，竟有165盆花。

我常常旅游，不在的时候就麻烦邻居照看我的植物。我意识到这个工作对他来说太繁重了，于是决定把花盆的数量减少到78盆。

我把我的花草送给朋友的时候，他们总是说：“只要拿一枝回去种就好了。”可是这并不能解决我的花盆数量太多的问题。你要么把整盆花拿去，要么不拿。

在生活中，我非常讨厌黑色魔鬼：二手烟。曾经有一段时间，抽烟的权利跟生活在干净卫生的环境里的权利被看得同等重要。我们没有法子，到处都得容忍。于是，我便在自己的私人范围——我的家里对付吸烟者。我绝不允许客人在我的公寓里抽烟。如果客人点着了香烟，我会要求他们灭掉。由于我没有烟灰缸，他们总是把烟掐灭在我的花盆里。

I once noticed a plant that had insects under its leaves, and I was about to treat it when I discovered it had recovered after "hosting" a cigarette butt.

I thought the tar could be an efficient repellent against red fleas, white flies and small worms.

A few days later, I brought a covered jar containing a little water to a colleague who was a smoker, and asked him to collect his cigarette butts for me, saying with a smile: "At least, you can make your bad habit useful!"

Though the mixture smells like hell after 48 hours, the product offers several advantages. First of all, it's free. Second, it's safe for the environment and harmless to the plants. Contrary to the result of inappropriate use of commercial pesticides, you can't damage your plants by spraying too much tar-juice on them.

The second time I asked my colleague for help, he said. "Every time I opened the jar to put a butt in it, I felt like fainting. When I realized there might be such a terrible smell inside my own body, I decided to quit smoking. Sorry! I can't help you.

I was proud of my request's result, although I had not done it on purpose. Scientific discoveries are often unexpected!

So, I continued to spot potential quitters, even when I had enough killer liquid for my plants. Without saying a word against their smoking habit, I gave them the same opportunity to realize what was happening in their lungs.

In less than one year, I had "saved" not only three smokers but their families and coworkers who had to inhale their secondhand poison.

For my double discovery – a bug-killer and a smoking-cessation method, don't you think I deserve a seat at the Academy?

有一次，我注意到一盆花的叶子下面有虫子。我正要整治，却发现放了烟头的植物都不治而愈了。

我觉得这可能是因为焦油可以驱除跳蚤、粉虱和其他小虫子的缘故。

几天以后，我把一个带盖的罐头瓶带到单位去，里面放了一点水，让一个抽烟的同事把香烟头放在那里面。我笑着对他说："你的坏习惯现在至少可以派一点用场了！"

48 小时以后，那瓶子里的味道就真是臭不可闻了。但是那种泡过烟头的水真是有好处：第一，免费；第二，对环境和植物都无害。与滥用杀虫剂不同，这种烟头水即使喷多了也不会伤害花草。

有一次，我让这个同事给我香烟头的时候，他说："我每次一打开那个瓶子放烟头，我就觉得要昏倒了。我意识到我自己的身体里也有这种可怕的味道，于是就决定戒烟了。现在我可帮不了你了。"

我很自豪，尽管是无心插柳，我的要求竟然收到了意外的效果。科学发现也常常出乎意料！

尽管杀虫烟头水已经足够了，我还是继续关注有可能戒烟的人。我不去批评的他们抽烟习惯，只让他们去体验肺里正在发生的情况。

在不到一年的时间里，我"拯救"了三名吸烟者，而且还将被迫吸他们二手烟的家人和同事解放出来。

为了我的这个双重发现——杀虫水和戒烟的方法，难道我不应该当选科学院院士吗？

Painting a pretty picture when speaking Chinese

I am a self-made woman in several fields: baking wonderful cakes; recycling Christmas cards; growing tomatoes in pots on the balcony; embroidering such a huge wedding trousseau when I was a girl that I had enough for three generations; repairing leaking pipes; adding a telephone on a house line; and learning languages.

Take Chinese, for instance. As I preach to others: Don't wait to be perfect in a language before you start to use it. This is what I did more than 20 years ago. Now, I always manage to make myself understood, though my language may not be perfect.

I am also a self-taught artist. My first painting in 1978 was a disaster. Of course, it could not have been a success, as I had chosen to draw a portrait of my daughter in watercolors, which didn't allow for any correction – unlike oils.

It took me another decade before I tried again. I've stuck to oil painting since.

Several Chinese artists who graduated from art schools encouraged me to continue. They said my style was free from the strict rules they were taught to follow, and now that they have become autonomous, they often find it difficult to free themselves and create their own styles.

However, I am not good at painting portraits and don't even want to try for the moment. I can only paint human faces that don't have to resemble anyone specifically.

The years 1988 and 2012 may be considered as the most productive periods of my painting career.

作画与说中文

我在好几个方面都能做到自力更生：会烤制可口的蛋糕，将旧圣诞卡变废为宝，在阳台上盆栽西红柿，在做姑娘的时候曾经绣过足够三代人用的结婚床单、毛巾、桌布等，自己修理泄露的管道，在房子里加装电话，还有学习语言。

比如学中文，我总告劝别人说，不要等到你的中文水平已经很好了才去使用。20 年前，我就是按这个方法学中文的。现在，虽然我的中文不是特别棒，我却能让别人听懂我的意思。

作画我也是自学的。1978 年，我画的第一幅画相当糟糕。我想给我的女儿画一幅水彩肖像，而水彩画可不像油画可以加以修改，自然没有画成。

又过了十多年，我才再次拿起画笔，从那时起就改学油画了。

有些美院毕业的中国画家鼓励我坚持画下去。他们说我的画不受任何学院规范的束缚。他们已经习惯成自然了，很难脱离巢臼去创立自己的风格。

可是，我不善于画肖像画，而且根本不想去尝试。我只能画谁也不像的人脸。

1988 到 2012 年是我的画作高产时期。

Recently, needing to restock my painting materials, I went to an art store. Upon seeing me, two idle vendors stopped chatting and asked what I wanted to buy. "*Hualian yanse*," I said.

As a good Italian, I always use my hands when I speak, so I probably gestured and pointed to my own face – which didn't help – when asking for what were literally "colors for painting the face".

As Chinese do when they find themselves in an uneasy situation, the two women spontaneously blushed. I thought about how I would paint a blushing person.

In the meantime, one lady answered: "*Duibuqi, women jiu mai huahua'r de cailiao.*" (Sorry, we sell only painting materials here.)

It took me 1.5 seconds to understand where the problem lay. Hualian means "to paint the face", which is synonymous with *huazhuang*, or "to make up" your face.

Sure enough, I knew they didn't sell cosmetics at the store. And I learned from my mistake that I had misused a word.

Strangely, at that moment, what came to my mind was what kind of materials do Peking Opera artists use when they perform "painted face" roles, and what would happen if a person used paint for walls on their skin?

All this happened in a fraction of a second.

I came back to reality, and in order to clear up the ladies' uneasiness, I asked them to teach me what I should have said. "*Pifuse, pifu yanliao*," they suggested.

最近，我去了一家美术用品商店，购买画画的材料。看见我进来，两个售货员停止了闲聊，问我想买什么。我说："画脸颜色。"

我是典型的意大利人，说话喜欢带手势。我指着自己的脸，告诉她们我要买的是"画脸用的颜料"，可是这种手势毫无用处。

就像中国人在身处困境时的表现一样，这两个女士的脸红了。当时让我联想到，如果我要画一张因窘迫而变红的脸，该怎么去画。

这时候，一个女士说："对不起，我们只卖画画的材料。"

过了几秒钟，我才明白了问题的所在，"画脸"跟"化妆"意思差不多。

我当然知道她们那里不卖化妆品，我意识到我用错词了。

当时我却在奇怪地想，京剧演员勾脸用的是什么材料，用漆墙的涂料画皮肤会是什么结果。

这一切都发生在一瞬间。

我的思绪又回到柜台上来。为了消除她们的不安，我让她们教我应该怎么说。她们告诉我应该说"皮肤色"或者"皮肤颜料"。

Resident not the same as citizen

Recently two topics have been warmly discussed among the expat community in China. One is the country's social security program covering foreign workers, which took effect in July last year. The other is permanent residency, which is sparingly granted to a small number of foreigners.

I belonged to the first group of 11 foreigners who were granted a Chinese permanent residence card in Beijing.

Seven persons of our group were *huaqiao*, or overseas Chinese who had emigrated from China and had become citizens of other countries, losing ipso facto their Chinese citizenship, as China doesn't recognize double citizenship.

Robert Mundell, the Canadian winner of Nobel Prize of Economy 1999, who had contributed to an economic theory and a monetary and financial system applicable to China, was one of us.

There were two ladies, one born in China and the other who came here before Liberation, in 1949. They were, in fact, permanent residents, but still had to go through yearly procedures to renew their visa.

Several people, Chinese as well as non-Chinese, think that if you have the permanent residence status, you automatically enjoy the benefits of a social security program, and that if you contribute to the latter, you should enjoy the former.

Permanent residence can be granted to individuals who are considered valuable talents necessary for China's development; to investors (and their families) of a substantial amount in the country's economy; to people who have made an outstanding contribution to the development of China and the cooperation between nations; and to an overseas member of a Chinese family, when the family is willing to take financial responsibility for that foreign relative.

居民并非公民

最近，在华的外国人中有两个热门话题。一是，从去年 7 月起，在华外籍工作人员可以办中国的社保了。二是，外国人可以获得永久居留身份，但获得这种资格的外国人现在很少。

在北京获得永久居民身份的第一批外国人有11个人,我是其中之一。

我们这批人中，有 7 个是华侨。因为中国不承认双重国籍，他们移民国外后获得其他国家的国籍，自动失去中国国籍。

我们当中还包括 1999 年获得诺贝尔经济学奖的加拿大人罗伯特·蒙代尔。 他对经济理论和货币金融体系理论做出了贡献，他的理论在中国得到了应用。

还有两位女士，一位出生于中国，另一位是 1949 年解放以前就来到了中国。他们是事实上的永久居民，但是每年都得办理签证延期。

有些人,包括中国公民及非中国公民都认为,如果有了永久居民身份,就可自动享有社会保险的福利；如果交社保，就应该享受到社保的福利。

永久居民身份可以授予几类人：中国发展所需要的特殊人才；在中国进行一定投资的投资人及其家庭成员；对中国发展和国际合作做出杰出贡献的人；中国家庭的外国成员（前提是这个家庭愿意为其提供经济支持）。

The permanent residence card allows the owner to get in and out of China without a visa. Therefore, some scientists and highly qualified professors, living abroad, became able to offer their services to their native country. The permit made it possible for them to come from Seattle, London or Singapore on the weekend, give a lecture at Peking University or Shanghai Fudan University on Monday, and return to their country the next day.

But the Chinese residence permit is not associated with any monetary advantages such as insurance, pensions or allowances. It consists only of the right to remain in the country, even without a work contract, which is the requirement otherwise.

"This is not fair!" complain many expats, who argue that China should support the housing, healthcare and transportation, among other things, of those who it deems deserving of permanent residence.

But China has a population of more than 1.3 billion. Its medical system and pension plan are still being developed. How can the State take charge of foreign citizens? China is not an immigration country. No one is forced to come to work here; if we come, it is because we want to come.

In countries where immigrants can apply for a green card after working for a certain number of years, the workers have first to be acknowledged as a "landed immigrant" so they have the right to work, and they must satisfy a series of conditions including contributing to social security programs.

I think it was a good decision for the government to include the foreign workers into the Chinese social net last year, even though it is not related to permanent residence. However, several expats I know said they didn't want to pay the extra charges.

China is not trying to profit from foreign workers. The system, still pending, is under international negotiations to avoid foreign workers

持有永久公民证件的人入境免于签证，方便一些居住国外的科学家和资深学者为国家提供服务。他们能够在周末从西雅图、伦敦或者新加坡来到中国，星期一在北京大学或者上海复旦大学举办讲座，第二天返回自己的国家。

中国的永久居民身份并不与经济利益挂钩，与保险、养老金或者别的福利都无关，仅仅表示赋予在这个国家居住的权利，即使没有工作也没有关系。但是，对于一个没有中国永久居民身份的外国人来说，有工作许可才能留在中国。

“这不公平！”很多居住在中国的外国人说。他们说，如果中国认为他们有资格享受永久居民身份，就应该给他们提供住房、医疗保险、交通等福利。

可是中国有十三亿人口，医保和养老金制度还在发展之中，国家怎么能为外国人埋单呢？中国不是一个移民国家，没有人被强迫来这里工作。如果我们来到这里，那是因为我们想来。

在有些国家，移民在工作若干年后，可以申请绿卡。但他们需要一开始就被认定为“入境移民”，这样他们就可以获得工作许可。当然，他们还必须满足一系列要求，包括缴纳社会保险。

去年,中国政府把外籍劳工纳入社会保险。虽然这和绿卡没有关系，我仍然认为这个政策很好，然而，我认识的一些在华外国人却表示不愿意缴纳额外的社保金。

中国并不是要从外籍劳工身上赚钱。目前，有一种尚未确定的安排

being doubly charged, and to arrange for the pension to be paid when one leaves the country or the payments to be redeemed.

In 2005, permanent residence was introduced by the Chinese government as a mean of luring foreign talent and attracting national scholars working overseas to return home often.

The 2010 census recorded nearly 600,000 foreigners living in China, and approximately 231,700 of them with work permits. According to China Daily, as of May 26, 721 foreigners had obtained permanent residence status in Beijing, and a total of 4,752 nationwide since 2005. Now that China is involving foreign workers in the social security system, it's normal that those who pay can benefit from medical insurance and a pension.

Retired foreigners with permanent residence are not included in the program. They have to pay taxes on any occasional earnings the same as any other citizen, but as they don't contribute to a Chinese social security plan, they obviously don't get any allowances. So remaining in China is a personal choice.

Some people say that there are many illegal workers in China because the work visa is too difficult to obtain. But if a foreigner is qualified for a post, and if there is no Chinese qualified to fill it, the State will issue a working visa to a foreigner according to the country's needs.

It's true that China doesn't provide permanent residence permits at large, and doesn't financially support those who are granted them, but as the country with the largest population in the world, China has to achieve its own development while taking care of its own population first.

I don't see any reason why China should expand its permanent residence program to more expats, or let those who have the status enjoy social security for free.

正处于谈判阶段，目的是避免外籍劳工在中国和本国缴纳双重社保，并在他们离开中国时可以领取退休金或者返还曾经缴纳的社保金。

2005 年，为了吸引国外人才，并让定居海外的华人学者常常回国进行学术活动，中国政府开始对外国人实施永久居民身份政策。

2010 年的人口普查表明，中国大约有 60 万外国人居住，其中大约有 231,700 人有工作许可。《中国日报》报道说，2005 年以来，北京已经有 721 名外国人士获得永久居留权，全国有 4,752 人。如今，中国已将外国劳工纳入社保系统，交纳社保金者将会享受医疗保险和退休金。

这个计划不包括有中国绿卡但已退休的外国人。这些外国人获得的临时性收入，都要像其他公民一样纳税。既然他们不缴纳社保金，也就没有社会保险。所以，是否留在中国，纯粹是个人选择。

有人说，在中国有很多外国人在非法打工，因为得到工作签证很难。但是如果某项工作中国人做不了，而外国人可以胜任，国家会根据需要发给该外国人工作签证。

的确，中国不随便给外国人永久居留权，对得到永久居留权的外国人也不提供财务上的承诺。中国是世界上人口最多的国家，不得不在发展过程中首先照顾本国国民。

我不认为中国应该放松对永久居留许可审批的控制，也不认为已获得永久居留权的外国人就该享受免费的社会保险。

No waste: good news!

The best news I heard since the 18th Congress of the Party in October 2012 was that the nation is encouraged to avoid wasting food. Several articles have been published since, with astronomic figures which should make some people blush for shame. It is said that the wasted food in China could feed 200 million people who still lack the necessary quantity and quality of food to keep good health, around 7 billion in the world.

The Chinese are hospitable, this is well known. To show their respects to their distinguished guests, they have developed the habit of ordering much more food than their guests can eat. If, at the end of the dinner, all the food has been eaten, the host could be criticized as being mean with money accordingly to the modern mentality of profligacy. The image of generosity is represented by a "fish", *yu*, homophone of another *yu* meaning not only abundance but surplus.

When invited to a restaurant by Chinese friends, I always try to stop them ordering too much. But they answer: "No matter, we can take the leftovers home."

Every foreigner who has been in China for a while knows the phrase *dabao* addressed to the waiters at the end of a dinner, meaning to wrap the remaining food so that it can be brought at home. If they really do, then I feel at ease.

This is a wonderful habit which I discovered in China, and I was told that China had learned from Germany, and later, from the United States. But I have not seen bringing back the leftovers in Western countries only very recently, except when I was young, in

喜闻节约厉行

2012 年 10 月中共十八大以来，我听到的最好的消息是反对浪费食物。有不少文章披露的相关数字足以让一些人脸红。世界上有 70 亿人，据说中国人浪费的粮食可以养活两亿人，这些人拥有的食物不足以维持身体健康。

众所周知，中国人好客。为了对贵宾表示尊敬，他们养成了给客人多点菜的习惯。如果一顿饭吃到最后什么都没有剩下，那主人会被认为花钱过于吝啬，有悖一掷千金的现代豪爽。这种大方豪爽可以用“鱼”来表示，“鱼”象征“裕”和“余”。

当中国朋友请我到餐馆吃饭的时候，我总是不让他们多点菜。他们总是说：“没关系，我们可以打包。”

在中国呆久了，外国人都知道“打包”的意思，那就是把没吃完的饭菜带回家去。如果中国人真这样做，那我倒也觉得释怀。

这是我在中国发现的一个非常好的习惯，听说中国人是从德国和美国学来的。但我最近才在西方国家看到把没吃完的菜带回家的现象。但我小时候也曾在加拿大看到过一种所谓的“狗袋”。人们说把没有吃完

Canada, there was a kind of "doggy bags" in which people said they carried the leftovers for their dogs, though being mocked by people who thought they would eat the food themselves at home.

Sometimes, after every guest has eaten one's content, the table seems to be ready for starting a meal. Some expensive dishes which were served late remain untouched.

I noticed that the Chinese waited for the foreigners to have left the dining room before asking to "*dabao*". So, I never skip a chance to strongly encourage them to follow this practice and avoid wasting.

When I was working with CCTV in the 1990s, at lunch time there was a huge help-yourself buffet for the employees, with extremely rich choice of food. Only a few yuan were taken from our card, and one could return to the buffet as many times as one wanted. But waste was forbidden, and those who would not empty their plate would be fined.

When I came to China in 1985 as a tourist, food was sufficient for the 10 customers at each table, and when we quit, all the dishes were empty. In 1989, I lived for three months in a university. Foreigners as well as locals used to have their meals at the school's cafeteria. The price of each dish was quite low, and each dish contained a reasonable individual quantity of food. More than often, students would leave the cafeteria without being completely full because they had not enough money for one more dish.

In the 1990s, students had no meat or fish in their ordinary diet, only bone soup with vegetables, and the rice was of low quality. Little by little, they started to go to restaurant once in a while, what has become usual today. I remember seeing students at an Origus buffet (set price, eat as much as you want), leaving an untouched plate of chicken wings on their table, among other leftovers.

In 2006, when "my Tibetan daughter" returned home in Yunnan for the first time after three years, I went to spend the Spring festival

的肉和骨头带回去喂狗，也有人笑话他们是要带回去自己吃。

有的时候，大家酒足饭饱之后，餐桌看起来仍然像是刚开席，后来上的菜价格不菲，却不再有人碰了。

我注意到，中国人总是等外国客人离开以后才要求打包。我也总是鼓励中国朋友这样做，免得浪费。

上个世纪 90 年代，我在央视工作。员工可以在自助餐厅吃饭，菜肴丰盛，可随意挑选。

我们吃饭只从饭卡上扣除几元钱。吃饭的人取多少次都行，但不可以浪费。如果盘子里有剩菜，就会被罚款。

1985 年，我到中国旅游时，吃饭每桌 10 人，饭菜足够。吃完饭的时候，大家的盘子都空了。1989 年，我在一个大学住了 3 个月。在那个大学里，外国人和中国人都在学校食堂就餐。饭菜价格很便宜，给的量也很足。但大学生们常常是没有吃饱就离开食堂了，因为他们没有钱多买一份菜。

到了 90 年代,学生们每天饮食里没有肉也没有鱼,只有蔬菜骨头汤。米饭的质量也不好。他们开始时不时地去饭馆吃饭。如今到饭馆吃饭则习以为常了。我记得在“好伦哥”自助餐厅看到学生吃饭，离开的时候桌子上还有一盘没有碰过的鸡翅。

2006 年,我的“西藏女儿”在外边上学 3 年后第一次回云南探亲时，

with her family, and her mother found she was so skinny. I discovered that when in Lhasa, four students took a bowl of rice each and shared only one dish, which they bought in turn.

In Italy, bread is considered as the symbol of the food. So it is sacred, and no one would waste bread. Thrift was a traditional virtue of the Chinese people. There was a time when every grain of rice was seen as the symbol of the farmers' labor in harsh conditions. Why shouldn't this moral quality come back?

In the West, the most serious wasting happens in hotel buffet for tourists or for business meetings and congresses. In Cuba, last year, where the choice of food was very limited, I realized that when too much is offered, people want to taste all and this causes huge waste. In China, waste happens at social banquets offered for welcoming, congratulations, New Year, thanking, etc.

Now that a public call has been launched by authorities, I wish that at high levels of government and business, hosts will have "an excuse" to become less lavish and put an end to food squandering. And so will lower levels think and do.

我赶过去和她们全家人一起过春节。妈妈觉得她太瘦了。在拉萨，我发现四个学生买了四碗米饭，但只分吃一个菜，那个菜他们轮流出钱买。

在意大利，食物的代表是面包。面包很神圣，没有人去浪费。节俭曾经是中国人的美德。中国人曾经一度认为粮食“粒粒皆辛苦”。为什么这种美德不能回归呢？

在西方，最大的浪费是饭店里给游客和商务会议准备的自助餐。去年在古巴，一个食品选择并不多的国家，我突然意识到如果食物提供太多，人们就什么都要尝尝，容易造成巨大浪费。在中国，在欢迎会、庆祝会、新年聚会和答谢宴会上容易出现浪费的情况。

现在官方号召节俭。我希望政府高层和商界在举办宴会的时候，主人正好可以“借口”从简办会，杜绝食物浪费现象，希望基层也自觉这么去做。

图书在版编目（CIP）数据

外国人，中国情：英汉对照/(加)李莎著；于岚译.
—北京：五洲传播出版社，2013.9
ISBN 978-7-5085-2605-8

Ⅰ. ①外… Ⅱ. ①李… ②于… Ⅲ. ①中国－概况
－英、汉 Ⅳ. ①D92

中国版本图书馆CIP数据核字(2013)第218752号

作　　者：Lisa Carducci（李莎·卡尔杜齐）
翻　　译：于　岚
漫画作者：庞　丽　李　旻　罗　杰（排名不分先后）
出 版 人：荆孝敏
责任编辑：张美景
装帧设计：李　杨

外国人，中国情

出版发行：五洲传播出版社
地　　址：北京市海淀区北三环中路31号生产力大楼B座7层
邮　　编：100088
电　　话：010-82005972，010-82007837
网　　址：www.cicc.org.cn
印　　刷：北京圣彩虹科技有限公司
开　　本：140×203mm 1/32
印　　张：5.5
版　　次：2013年9月第一版第一次印刷
书　　号：ISBN 978-7-5085-2605-8
定　　价：69.00元